LENT:
A JOURNEY TO
RESURRECTION

**Prayers
and Reflections for
the Penitential Season**

Rawley Myers

OUR SUNDAY VISITOR

Nihil Obstat:
Rev. Edward M. Hoffman, Chancellor
Censor Librorum

Imprimatur: ✝James V. Casey, D.D.
Archbishop of Denver
October 3, 1983

The Nihil Obstat and Imprimatur are official declarations that a book or pamphlet is free of doctrinal or moral error. No implication is contained therein that those who have granted the Nihil Obstat or Imprimatur agree with the contents, opinions or statements expressed.

Library of Congress Catalogue No: 83-63084
ISBN 0-87973-605-4

Printed in the United States of America

*dedicated to
these priests,
all close to
the Sacred Heart,
who have influenced
me the most —*
*Msgr. Thomas Kealy, Msgr. Patrick Healy,
Father Daniel Lord, S.J., Father John Howe,
Father John Flynn, Father Michael Kavanagh,
and Father Gene Kalin.*

Contents

Preface

Lent is a special time to be with Jesus so we can be like Jesus. We are given each year this sacred season to draw closer to Christ in order that we may know Him better and love Him more. To imitate Jesus, of course, is the very heart of our faith; it is what Christianity is all about.

A person can gain heaven without knowing many things in religion. He does not have to know how many candles to light for Benediction or the names of the various vestments the priest wears at Mass. But no Christian can gain eternal life without knowing Christ. The word Christian means a Christ-follower. No one can follow someone he does not know. We must, then, strive to know Christ, for to know Him is to love Him.

Lent gives us this opportunity. During Lent we imitate Christ, who spent 40 days in prayer and penance in the desert. We are given 40 days now to prepare for the great and wonderful feast of Easter, the Resurrection of Our Lord. But we are not just preparing for Christ's Resurrection, we are preparing for our own. After our death we will live again and be judged by God.

If we know Christ then, we will have nothing to fear. So let us use these precious days to prepare ourselves by prayer and penance; in this way we will grow closer to Jesus, our dearest Friend.

A word about this book and how to use it: It begins with prayers and reflections for each day of Lent. The first thing you will notice is that there are 46 sets of prayers and reflections for only 40 days of Lent. That is because the six Sundays of Lent, including the two Sundays of the Passion, are not, properly speaking, a part of Lent. They are the Lord's days, oases in the desert of our journey. We include them in our prayers and reflections to sustain the mood of pilgrimage.

Next there is a section of Bible readings, additional prayers and reflection-starters. The preceding section may be all you'll need on your first trip, but when you become a seasoned traveler you will want to make your own spiritual excursions. The simple thoughts in the first section may not always be enough for you, so I've included some additional suggestions.

The richest source of meditation is God's own word in the Holy Bible, so I have suggested some weekday readings from the New Testament. Then the thoughts of various Christian writers and prayers from the writings of the saints may be all you'll need to assemble your own reflections day by day.

In the third part I have included some familiar prayers and devotions to refresh you. The Way of the Cross is a valuable Lenten devotion, especially during Holy Week, and there is no greater literature expressing sorrow than the penitential psalms you will find in "A Lenten Psalter." Finally there is a long meditation on the Passion of Christ and the implication of the Resurrection. Take it in small bites, letting the Passion seep into your being during Holy Week — and on Easter you will rise refreshed with the risen Lord, with whom you will have completed a long and loving journey.

— Rawley Myers

1

A 40-Day Journey

*Daily Prayers
and Reflections*

Beginning the Journey

Ash Wednesday

Reflection

"Remember, man, you are dust and to dust you will return" (Ash Wednesday liturgy).

These sobering words of the priest as he puts ashes on our foreheads force us to reflect on the fact that we are going to die. Death comes to every person. We are all mortal. All the great world leaders of our childhood are gone, and, as sure as the night follows the day, we will follow them to the grave. Probably sooner than we think right now. We know that the longest life is very short, and after death one is remembered for a while by a few friends and then as time goes on the memory fades and we will be forgotten like the rest.

What happens after death? Jesus is our divine guide who came from heaven to tell us about the mystery of life and about the even more puzzling mystery of death. Jesus tells us that death is the door through which we pass from this life into the next life. This world and this life give way to another world and another life. We are here on earth to prepare for eternal life. We are given this time to grow in love so that after death we will go to a place of love, which we call heaven. It is a place of love because it is God's home and, as St. John tells us, God is Love. No one without love would be happy there, C.S. Lewis wrote. An unloving person couldn't stand such a loving place and so would leave heaven of his own accord. The egotistically selfish individual will walk out of heaven, Lewis said, but outside of heaven — is hell.

Heaven is for those who strive to love in this life. People who refuse to grow in love, who reject Jesus and His message of love, grow in selfishness, which is a perversion of love. They turn the love that God gives them inward instead of outward.

The love of God, given to each of us, is supposed to flow through the heart, like a delightful, joyful, sparkling mountain stream. It is to go out to others. Love is to share. But the selfish person dams up his heart and will not let love pass through. Like a miser he keeps it all for himself, and love, which is to flow out like a lively stream, then becomes stagnant and sour, a pond of dead water.

So after death, God gives the person striving for love in this life a place of love in eternity, heaven. And He gives the selfish person, who spends all his love on himself, precisely what he wants too. He gives the egotistical individual the things that he loves the most — himself. He is imprisoned in a dungeon of mirrors where all he can see is himself — and that is hell.

Prayer

Jesus, I love You. You know that I do. Sometimes when I look at the crucifix and see Your agony and all You endured for me — Your head crowned with thorns, Your back nearly broken from the beating, Your hands and feet nailed and Your face and body covered with blood — sometimes when I think of how You suffered for me, tears come to my eyes.

But, alas, that is only sometimes. Sometimes, I must confess, I don't feel anything when I pray. I am so distracted, thinking of everything else. Sometimes, Lord, You seem so far away, and sometimes spiritual things seem remote and distant.

Dear Lord, I am such an earth-bound creature. Forgive me. As the Apostles said (see Mark 11:1), "Lord, teach us to pray." Help me when I pray to lift up my mind and heart to You. Reach out Your hands, dear Jesus, as You did so often when You walked in the world and heal me; touch my mind and heart and heal me so that I will not be so selfish, so unloving. Touch my soul, dear Savior, so I can cast out anxiety and think of You. Give me joy of heart, like the joy You gave to St. Francis of Assisi, so that I will worry less about possessions and rejoice more in Your presence. Please help me and heal me, dear Jesus. Amen.

Thursday After Ash Wednesday

Reflection

Death, for one who strives to grow in love, holds no fear. Jesus told us that for such people death is not the end of life but truly the beginning of life. Christian death is the beginning of a joy and love and peace in heaven that this world cannot give and we cannot even begin to imagine. St. Paul had a vision of heaven, and he tried to explain it, but could not. Human words are not adequate to tell of the splendor of eternal glory. Paul, as we know, was never at a loss for words, but he was this time. He simply gave up, saying, "Eye has not seen nor ear heard, nor has it entered into the heart of man, what God has prepared for those who love him" (1 Corinthians 2:9).

Death for the Christ-follower is like coming out of a cave into a stunningly beautiful, bright, sunny spring afternoon.

Death for a friend of Jesus is a homecoming, coming home to heaven, the home of our Father. This world is not our true home. One of the first things we come to realize here is that all is constantly changing. Life here is too ephemeral and superficial. Our hearts long for permanent peace and love and happiness, not for a day or many days, but forever. In this, one feels, our hearts are more knowledgeable than we are. For from time to time we all experience a restlessness of heart. Everything apparently is fine, but still we are not content. I think this is because our hearts are homesick, reaching out for our true home of heaven. As St. Augustine said, "Our hearts are restless, O Lord, until they rest in Thee."

When one who loves Jesus dies, instead of sadness there is joy. For just on the other side of the door of death, our dearest Friend is standing, waiting with arms outstretched to greet and welcome us and embrace us. What a glorious day that will be when Jesus calls us by name and smiles at us and so kindly puts His arms around us and takes us home with Him to greet our family and friends. Oh yes, they will be there, the people we loved so much in this life who now are gone. One of the greatest joys of heaven will be to be once again with our dear ones. What pure happiness that will be. And to be with them forever in heaven, where there is joy and goodness and love and peace without end. God is so good to us; His lavish generosity is wonderful beyond words.

Prayer

Help me, dear Jesus, to be more grateful. Help me to start every prayer with a "Thank You." I am always asking for things; so rarely do I express gratitude. So many of my prayers are "gimme" prayers: gimme this, gimme that, gimme something else. And when You do give me things, I often forget the most basic rule of common courtesy: I fail to show any appreciation. How rude and discourteous I am. If I give a little kid a nickel, I am very upset if he does not thank me. But You, O God, give me everything. Every breath I breathe is Your gift; every beat of my heart is Your gift. I am grateful, Lord. Please help me to thank You more often.

Dear Jesus, take from my heart my pride, which blocks the door and will not let You enter. Give me the gift of humility, which throws open the door wide to welcome You with open arms. You can't enter a heart hardened by pride. You can only stand outside and knock at the door — in vain. But You love a humble heart. It is not all cluttered up with selfish concerns, and so there is room for You to come in.

Come, Lord. Come into my heart and abide with me, for when You come there is joy and love. Come, Lord Jesus, come. Amen.

Friday After Ash Wednesday

Reflection

St. Mark tells us that after his baptism by John, Jesus went into the desert to pray. "The heavens opened and the Spirit, like a dove, came down and rested upon him. There was a voice too, out of Heaven, 'You are my beloved Son; in you I am well pleased.' Thereupon, the Spirit sent him out into the desert, and in the desert he spent forty days and forty nights." (See Mark 1:10-13.)

Jesus was a man of prayer. He lived nearly 30 years in prayer before He began to preach. Prayer is the dominant theme that runs through the whole Gospel story, like the basic melody of a great symphony. We frequently overlook this because the miracles are so dazzling, but on almost every page it tells of prayer. Jesus went aside to pray; He went to the mountainside to be alone to pray; He spent the whole night in prayer.

What did Jesus do most in Nazareth growing up? He prayed. He learned to pray at His Mother's knee; some of His first words were little prayers. No doubt Joseph taught Him prayers as he took Him for walks in the countryside to show Him all the beauty and wonders of nature for which he praised God. The holy family daily prayed together and weekly went to the synagogue. The Youth prayed as He worked with the wood in the carpenter shop. In the silence there He had ample opportunity to pray as He made a table for a poor widow or toys for little children. When His work was done He could escape to the hills and be by himself. There He could think about God. Watching the magnificent sunset, He would give thanks and glory to God for this spectacular gift.

And then in a cave in the desert for 40 days He prayed before beginning His public teaching.

If prayer was so important to Jesus, it must also be important in our lives, for we are His disciples. We must pray often, as Jesus did. And we must realize what real prayer is: thinking of Jesus. Too many people in prayer spend all their time asking for things. But we don't have to tell God what He already knows. He is aware of our difficulties. He knows too that Uncle Ned has a bad back and that Aunt Jane is in the hospital. Of course, we are to ask for our needs in prayer, for Jesus said, "Ask, and you will receive" (John 16:24). (Cardinal Newman reminds us that Jesus said, "You will receive," but He did not say "at once" — so one should persevere in prayer.)

Yes, we are to ask but not all the time, not a long litany of our wants. Prayer is thinking of Jesus, and if we only think of Him His love will warm our hearts.

Prayer

Dear Jesus, here I am. I want to thank You for the many blessings that You give me and my loved ones every day. You are so gracious and generous, and often I fail to stop and thank You, so now I especially wish to express my gratitude to You. Thank You for the great gift of life that You have given me. It is a free present to me on Your part. I did nothing to deserve life — yet here I am. Thank You. You could have made a million other people besides me, but in Your great love for me, You have given me life. Thank You very much, Lord.

I know You said that the best way to thank You is by

deeds. And so I ask You to help me today to help someone else in Your name. Maybe just a smile or a kind word is all that I can give away — but You love to have us do whatever we can, small as it may be. You want us to cheer up others and brighten their day and make their burdens a little lighter. Help me to do this for You today — You have done so much for me.

Thank You for sunshine, for flowers, for mountains, for sunsets, for smiling babies and laughing children. Thank You, Lord, for life and love and home and family. Amen.

Saturday After Ash Wednesday

Reflection

Prayer is so important because in prayer we meet Jesus and visit with Him. Sometimes we are not always aware of this, but Jesus is always there when we pray. Sometimes in prayer we cannot think of anything to say. Then we can just sit there quietly in silence. Good friends often do that. They do not have to talk; they just enjoy being together. And with Jesus one does not have to be babbling all the time. Someone has said, "Friends enjoy wasting time together." So with Jesus we do not always need words; we can just enjoy being with Him.

Our Lord did not say a great deal about prayer. He taught in a better way, by example. Jesus was, above all, a man of prayer. He was always praying. That should be reason enough for us to pray frequently.

When Jesus did speak of prayer, as in the Sermon on

the Mount, He told us we do not have to use many words. God doesn't count them or weigh them. Nor should we be like the pagans, He said, and think we can impress God with big words. He does not have a ruler to measure how long our words are. What He wants is that we pray from our heart. (See Matthew 6:5-15.)

There are many ways to pray, to be sure. Every time you do a good deed, it is a prayer. Every time you read the Gospel, it is a prayer. Every time you go to Mass or receive a sacrament, it is a prayer.

A person can pray by reading prayers out of a prayer book, if he does so thoughtfully. One can pray by reciting memorized prayers, but do not rattle through these a mile a minute, and do not just say words with your lips while your mind is a million miles away. In prayer it is much more important to engage the mind than to engage the tongue. One shouldn't be like a parrot, saying words without thinking.

Some people have mistaken notions about prayer. They think that you can only pray in church, and they don't go to church very much so they don't pray very much. Nonsense! You can pray anywhere, anytime. You can pray driving the car — but I would not advise you then to be reading prayers out of a prayer book. You can pray doing the dishes, taking a walk, mowing the lawn, minding the children. Some think you have to be on your knees to pray, but the adage tells us, "He who prays on his knees prays very little." Your position in prayer is not important — visiting with Jesus is what is important.

The great St. Teresa of Avila said you should pray any way that you are comfortable. When you visit a friend you sit down and talk. In prayer you should do the same, for you are conversing with your best Friend.

Prayer

Grant me Your gracious blessings, O Lord. I am Your humble servant. I can do nothing without Your help. Come to me, Jesus, and bring me Your graces, so that I can grow in love, as You wish.

Bless my family. All of us need Your assistance, dear Lord. Bless my relatives and friends and all who are sick and all who are in need and all who are dying today and all the poor souls.

Bless our country, O Lord. America needs our prayers. You have been so kind in giving us this good and gracious land. America is the garden spot of the world. Thank You for giving me life here in this prosperous country; so many people in the world go to bed hungry. Thank You for the freedom we enjoy; most of the people in the world are governed by tyrants. You have smiled on our country and I am grateful. Yet we have our problems, and we need Your blessings. Give our officials wisdom to know how to lead us and justice in all that they do. Enlighten them and guide them to make right decisions. Reward them for their service to our country. And give our nation peace in our times and in all times. Amen.

First Week

First Sunday of Lent

Reflection

If someone new moves into our neighborhood, how do we get to know that person? There are various ways, of course, but the best way is just to go over and knock on the door and introduce yourself and sit down and visit with him. One learns more about a person from meeting him than from reading a book about him. Woodrow Wilson said he would rather visit with an author than read his book.

Since prayer is visiting with Jesus, it is the best way of getting to know Him. We can just sit down and talk to Him in our own words; as the old lady said, "I'm jest gonna set down and have a little talk with the Lord." When we talk with Jesus in our own words, we don't have to worry about distractions in prayer. When you use your own words, you have to think about what you are saying.

Talking to Jesus is easy. Tell Him what is in your heart. Some people think prayer is complicated; indeed, they spend more time getting ready for prayer than in praying. Other people in prayer get themselves into such an uncomfortable position that the pain is all they can think of — they do not think of Jesus at all. We should not confuse prayer and penance. Certainly prayer should not be penance; it should be a time of joy. If you want to practice penance, that is wonderful, but do not do so during prayer. In fact, if you want a good penance — be kind to people, smile at people, be patient with people when they are impatient with you. That is penance enough for anyone. But in prayer you should be happy, for you are with your best Friend. Postpone your penance for another time; don't get yourself all miserable, your body contorted like a pretzel.

Just visit with Jesus. If you lived in Palestine in the time of Our Lord and you were walking along a path and, turning a corner, you came upon Jesus sitting alone beneath a tree, what would you do? You would go up to Him, of course. And you would speak with Him. What would you say? I don't think you would rush up and say, "I believe in God, the Father almighty, Creator of Heaven and earth, etc., etc." The Creed is a beautiful prayer, and there is a time and place for it. But I think if you met Jesus person to person, face to face, you would forget all about memorized prayers and you would pour out your heart to Him. Do it now. He is with you. He wants you to visit with Him without fancy words. Talk to Him as you would talk to a friend. He is your Friend, you know, your dearest, closest Friend, and He delights in visiting with you. He longs to be with you because He loves you so much, and you invite Him to be with you when you pray — and when you invite Him, He is always there.

Prayer

Like most people, Lord, I think too much about myself. I think a lot about my aches and pains and sometimes feel sorry for myself. How foolish is self-pity, especially when

I look around in the world and see so many people so much worse off than I am. I recall the Arabian proverb, "I complained because I had no shoes, until I saw the man who had no feet." I am so fortunate. Thank You.

Thanks for my loved ones, my family and friends. Be good to them and help them. Bless them today and every day. Take care of them, Lord. And dear Blessed Mary, I ask you, my Mother in heaven, to protect my loved ones in a very special way. Place them under the blue mantle of your love, Mary.

Please help too those who are sick, Lord. They need Your special strength to endure their pain. Help them to be patient when they feel restless, to have hope when they feel discouraged. Smile on all who are sick today, Lord, and take care of them and give them a little extra hope and a little less suffering. Amen.

Monday, First Week of Lent

Reflection

St. Thomas Aquinas said he learned more in five minutes on his knees in prayer than from all the great books he had ever read. He was a great and brilliant man, and because he was great he knew that the way to draw closer to Christ, the only thing that really matters, is through prayer. All the saints were people who prayed, like Jesus. Prayer is the key to heaven.

Sometimes in prayer we get discouraged. We pray for something and we do not get it. Well, this much we know. Every prayer is answered. There is no such thing as an unanswered prayer. But God does not always answer our prayers in our way — He answers them in a better way. As Archbishop Fulton Sheen said, "God doesn't always give us what we want, but He always gives us what we need." We should pray, and leave the answer up to God. His way is the best way, even if at the time we with our small minds cannot see it.

Suffering too is prayer. As the sign I once saw in a church said, "Don't waste pain." When you offer your pain up to God, it is a prayer and a most beautiful one.

The greatest prayer we have is the Mass, for at Mass we pray with Jesus and He prays with us. There is no prayer that can compare with that. Our prayers alone are pleasing to God, to be sure, but they are, after all, like the little lispings of a kindergarten kid. At Mass, however, Jesus takes our feeble, tiny efforts and unites them with His prayers.

Imagine that you are in church kneeling and praying, and suddenly, wonder of wonders, Jesus is kneeling there praying beside you. That is what the Mass is. And that is why the Mass is infinitely pleasing in the sight of the Father, for it is the prayer of Jesus, and He allows us to pray with Him.

The Mass is the worship that Christ gave us. It is not a ceremony made up by a monk in the Middle Ages. Christ gave us the Mass, which is a reenactment of what He did at the Last Supper. And after He consecrated the Holy Eucharist, He said, "Do this in memory of me" (Luke 2:19). That is why we have the Mass. Jesus told us to do this. And isn't being a Christian being one who does what Christ tells us?

The glory of the Mass is that Jesus is present. We don't go to Mass for the music or the ceremony or the sermon;

we go to Mass to be with Jesus. He promised to be there, and He promised us, if we come to Him, that He will bless us in a most special way. We all need His blessings very much. Someone who says or implies he does not need God's help is fooling himself, and the proverb states well, "There is no fool like the fool who fools himself." If we are honest with ourselves, we must say we need the blessings of Jesus more than anything, and these blessings await us in abundance at Mass.

Prayer

Here I am, Lord. I want to pray for others today. I am sure that if I pray for others, You will take care of me. I feel, to paraphrase Your words, that if we seek first the needs of others, then all other things will be given to us.

So today, Jesus, I ask You to help those who are troubled. Some people are sick in body, and some are sick in mind, and some are sick in soul. Help troubled people to see that You are the answer to all their problems. This sounds so simple, but it is true. Because it sounds so simple, most people will do anything else — except pray. And they continue to worry and be troubled. Give them, Lord Jesus, the wisdom to know that You and You alone can heal them and give them courage. Enlighten the people who are anxious, and draw them closer to You. Teach them to pray, as You taught the Apostles to pray. And when they learn to pray they will find You, and with You they will find healing. Amen.

Tuesday, First Week of Lent

Reflection

Our Lord every day is seeking to lead us toward something better, but we, unfortunately, through selfishness, frequently block the action of His graces in our soul. We must strive to overcome our pride, for we will only change for the better when our hearts are right. That is why Jesus said to us, "Learn of me, for I am humble and gentle of heart" (Matthew 11:29). We are to follow the example of Christ, who was always wonderfully unselfish.

Jesus said we are not to fret for worldly things; too many possessions distract us from the things of God. We must, rather, go against the grain and follow Christ, in opposition to our openly materialistic world, where money is king. We must not be preoccupied with money and what it can buy, but must put up with our lack of it and endure our discomforts cheerfully. As an old philosophy professor said, "You shouldn't have all you want, and you shouldn't want all you have." A certain detachment in regard to worldly goods is good for us, for then we will receive the blessings Christ promised to the "poor in spirit" (Matthew 5:3; see Luke 6:20).

St. Francis of Assisi was one of the happiest individuals who ever lived — and one of the poorest. He started out in life wishing to have many possessions and every kind of pleasure; his father was a well-to-do merchant, and Francis seemed determined to spend all his Father's money; the youth loved fine clothes and festive parties and the best of everything. But he came to realize that true happiness is not in external things, but in the heart.

Rich men, indeed, are often the most unhappy people. Francis then exchanged his expensive apparel for a gunnysack with a rope tied around his waist. He became a beggar for the Lord. Yet in giving up all, he found all. Francis found that in throwing overboard the excessive baggage of life, he had made room in his heart for Jesus and joy. He walked down the road with a song in his heart. He found that with Jesus one needs nothing more.

We ordinary people cannot be as heroic as Francis, who was one of God's most noble saints, but the lesson is there. Do not get bogged down with too many possessions. Do not become preoccupied with buying things all the time. Leave room in your heart for Jesus, if you wish true happiness.

Our Lord is indeed each day seeking to lead you to something better. The world wants to pull you down, and to junk up your heart with garbage. But Christ points out that there is something far more beautiful in life than the trinkets and gadgets that the world has to offer. Jesus wants you to be an unselfish, truly wonderful individual, noble and loving, joyous and gentle. Jesus wants to get you out of your rut; He wants you to wake up, as Francis woke up one day, and see all the fine things you can do for others, and be happy.

Prayer

Dear Lord, don't let me be selfish in prayer and think always of myself and my needs. Other people have greater needs. And I am sure that when I pray for others, You will take care of me.

Please help those who are sick. And help troubled people. So many have such big problems. They need Your assistance, O Lord. You can answer their difficulties; let them turn to You. Too many individuals try everyone and everything else except You. Help them to see that You are our Guide in life. You will show us the way, if we let You. We really can do nothing without You. But with You things happen that we cannot explain. As the angel said to Mary: "Nothing is impossible with God" (Luke 1:37).

Shower Your blessings and graces on our sick and troubled world. Let there be peace in our day, and in every age. Turn back the hatred of evil forces; support and guard the peacemakers, so that never again will the world get involved in killing and war. You, Lord, are the Prince of Peace. I pray for Your help. With humble heart I plead that there will be, as Pope Paul VI said, "No more war — war never again!" Amen.

Wednesday, First Week of Lent

Reflection

In proportion as we profess ourselves to be Christians, our work is to help others. For that was the work of Christ, and we are His followers. This is what the word Christian means, a Christ-follower. We are to imitate Jesus.

Do you help others? Some people think this means to be a missionary and go halfway around the world and work with the natives in the stinking, rotting jungle; others think it means to convert thousands or to be a great preacher, holding a huge congregation in awe as one explains great theological mysteries. Many such people believe that since they cannot do any of these great things, they don't have to do anything. But, of course, this is not true. To be sure, we can't do tremendous things, because we are little people, but Jesus wants us nevertheless to do something. After all, the greatest saints in heaven, Joseph and the Blessed Mother, did ordinary things. They were not great preachers or convert-makers or missionaries. They lived in a small town and did small things. But that is just the point. Jesus loves them so much because they did what they could, small as it might be.

Can you imagine the Blessed Mother in Nazareth saying, "All I can do here is help my neighbors; so since I can't do more than that, since I can't do great and earth-shaking things, I'll do nothing"? She never thought like that at all. She was such a beautiful person, great or small meant nothing to her — that was for the proud of heart. She simply saw people who were in need and reached out to help them.

When the angel at the Annunciation told Mary that her aged cousin Elizabeth was with child, Mary went at once to assist her (see Luke 1:36ff). Here it had been related to her that she was to be the Mother of the Messiah; she had received the greatest honor that could come to anyone. Did she think of how privileged she was? No. All she knew was that Elizabeth needed help, and, even though she lived a long way away, she started out almost at once to be with her cousin.

Can you think of anyone who came to the little home there at Nazareth being turned away by Mary? Impossible. Our minds cannot even begin to imagine such a thing. Let us strive then to be more like her, for Mary was the first Christian and the best Christian. And in trying to be like her, we please Jesus most of all. We ask her help so that we may imitate her beautiful example. We cannot think of her talking a great deal; we think of her, rather, as a woman of silence, but one who never failed to be there when anyone was in need.

We feel we can turn to her in prayer and ask her assistance, for surely just as she never refused anyone who came to her for help when she was on earth, she will not refuse anyone now, for in heaven she is even closer to her beloved Son.

Prayer

Blessed Mother, we have confidence in your help. The great St. Bernard wrote the beautiful prayer, the *Memorare*, in which he said, "Remember, O most gracious Virgin Mary, that never was it known that anyone who fled to your assistance . . . was left unaided." These are powerful words, but they are the words of a saint. And so, with the confidence of St. Bernard, we turn to you. We ask your graces.

We remember that when you appeared to St. Catherine Labouré, you appeared with outstretched hands, and in your hands there were many jewels. Some of them were bright and sparkling, and others were dull and tarnished. St. Catherine asked you the meaning of this vision, the picture we see now on the Miraculous Medal. And you answered, "These jewels represent the graces I have to give to people. The bright and beautiful jewels are the blessings I have given away, but the dull and tarnished jewels represent the many graces I have to give to men — but which no one bothers to ask for."

Let me reflect on this sobering, tragic thought. We miss so many graces which you offer, because we are too busy to ask for them. Amen.

Thursday, First Week of Lent

Reflection

Can you say to Christ, "I am Your disciple, doing what You want me to"? Every true Christian should say this. To be a Christian, after the heart of Christ, means doing more than just the bare minimum of good example. Even the pagans do that.

The real Christ-follower reaches out to help his neighbor in need. Jesus said we must "love God . . . and love our neighbor" (Matthew 22:37-39; Mark 12:30-31; Luke 10:27) if we wish to gain eternal life. The inquirer then asked, "But who is my neighbor?" (Luke 10:29). And Jesus told the Parable of the Good Samaritan (see Luke 10:30-37). There is a Jewish proverb that says, "Ask a rabbi a question and he will tell you a story." Jesus was a Jewish rabbi, a teacher, and He often told stories. And one of the most meaningful is His story of the Good Samaritan.

We recall that Jesus was talking to Jews, and the Samaritans were like the Arabs today. We know the Jews and the Arabs cannot get along with one another; well, neither could the Jews and the Samaritans at the time of Christ. It must have galled His Jewish audience then when he chose to make the Samaritan the hero of His story.

In the parable a Jew is going on a trip from Jerusalem to Jericho. He is attacked by a band of ruthless robbers who beat him up, take everything he has and leave him half dead in the ditch.

Along comes a priest. But he passes the poor man by. Perhaps the priest was rushing off to preach a sermon on charity. At any rate, he went on. Next came a levite, a kind of deacon, and he also passed by. Maybe he did not have time to practice charity because he was on the way to a meeting to talk about charity.

At last a third person, a foreigner, a Samaritan, came along and saw the man in distress, and he went to him at once, even though he was a Jew and an enemy of the Samaritans. He climbed down into the ditch and gave him first aid. He then got him on his donkey and took him to an inn (there were no hospitals in those days) and looked after him. When the injured man was better, the Samaritan had to continue his journey, which he had already delayed for some days. But he was extremely generous. He told the innkeeper to look in on the man and take him his meals and do anything else that might be needed — and the Samaritan would pay him for all this also.

So after this parable the answer to the question, "Who is my neighbor?" was evident. Anyone in need is our neighbor. Go to him; help him. Don't ask a lot of questions. Don't have him fill out a long form. Don't ask him his religion or political affiliation or ethnic background. These things are not important. What is important is that we are all children of God and we must help our brothers and sisters in need.

Prayer

Jesus, I am so small of mind. I usually only think about myself and my family and my little circle of friends. But I should do more, I know. I want to do Your work, O Lord. The amazing thing is that when we help our neighbor — we are helping You. For You said, Lord, "I was hungry, and you gave ME to eat; lonely, and you visited ME." And when the astonished listeners asked, "When did we see you hungry, thirsty, naked, a stranger and in prison, and help you?" You replied, dear Jesus, "Whenever you did it for the least of my little ones, you did it for ME" (Matthew 25:35-40).

If I lived when You lived in the world, I would have wanted to do things for You to repay Your great love. But the fact is that I can do this very thing here and now. Whenever I help anyone, I am helping You, O Lord.

Bless me to be like the religious sister in the leper colony. The government official inspecting the place saw her changing bandages on a horribly deformed leper and doing it with a smile. Afterwards he said, "Sister, I wouldn't do that kind of work for a million dollars." And Sister said, "Neither would I." But she added: "I can do this because every time I see a patient, I see Christ." Amen.

Friday, First Week of Lent

Reflection

By leading us away from fear and turning our minds toward the goodness of God, Christ teaches us hope. By fixing our eyes on the love of God, our Father, He increases our love.

Jesus showed love in all that He did. He didn't just talk about it; He daily, unselfishly and with gentleness, spent His time helping others. How gracious and kind He was. We are His disciples; we must carry on His work. That is what a disciple does. Do you do good for Jesus, or do you turn your back on Him and ignore Him most of the week?

By the way we treat our neighbor, we will know if we are true followers of Jesus. Jesus said, "By this will all men know that you are my disciples, that you have love for one another" (John 13:35). Love is the mark of the Christian, not sitting in the first pew in church. In fact, if you go to church often and do not help your neighbor in need, what kind of a Christian are you? Certainly not one after the heart of Christ.

In order that we may be more like Jesus, He sends us the Holy Spirit, as He did to the first Apostles on Pentecost. The Holy Spirit, the Love of God, comes to our souls and gives us light and strength, the same kind of understanding and courage given to the Apostles. We are enriched with a new heart and a new spirit; we are enlightened and fortified. So no one is alone in his efforts to be like Christ in giving away love. Jesus and His Holy Spirit are with us.

We are to be Christ's apostles in the world today; we are the modern bearers of the "good news." The task is great and we are weak, but then we are no weaker than were the Apostles, and God did wondrous things through them. When we are fearful, we recall that the Apostles were not less fearful. But they came to see that with God they could spread the "good news." St. Paul said, "I can do all things in Him who strengthens me" (Philippians 4:13).

Jesus told us that with faith we could move mountains. Worldly people think Christians are fools. We are — fools for Christ — just as the first great Christians were fools for Christ. But we are not so foolish as to think we can do anything for Christ without Christ. On the other hand, we know that with Him we can do wonders, if we open our hearts to Him. Jesus told us that if we but open our hearts,

He and the Father will come. "We will come to him and make our abode with him" (John 14:23). We need nothing more. When God comes to us, He brings wisdom and kindness, the two things we most badly need and can never get on our own. If we let God take over our hearts, we will grow in love and we will want to do good things and we will be happy. As the saints have said, "To serve God is to reign."

Prayer

Dear Lord, we are so helpless, we human beings. But to know that is a step forward. Humility is the beginning of wisdom. Too many times we are very proud and think we can solve all our difficulties by ourselves. And in our preoccupation with problems, we forget You, Lord. And that is our worst mistake. We can really do nothing without You, and we are foolish to try. We know, of course, that "God helps those who help themselves." But we are also aware of the words of St. Teresa: "Work as if everything depends on you; pray as though everything depends on God." Our efforts must begin with prayer or we will fail. The psalmist says, "In vain does the guard keep watch, if the Lord does not guard the city" (Psalm 127:1).

Teach us to know that You are standing beside us and want to assist us. Why must we always be like little stubborn, headstrong children and want to do everything our way? How foolish, how childish. Teach us to turn to You and pray to You, and spend more time praying than doing, and we will accomplish our purpose. Otherwise all our efforts are in vain and, even though we may gain worldly success, we will fail in the long run. Amen.

Saturday, First Week of Lent

Reflection

"Come to me, all you who are weary, and I will refresh you," Jesus said (Matthew 11:28). Life at times becomes very difficult for all of us, and we need Jesus to comfort us. We should put all our trust in Him. We should let Him sustain us. He wants very much to help, you know. He wants us to turn to Him so He can look after us and take care of us. Our troubles start when we forget Christ and attempt to do everything on our own. Alone we are helpless. But if we have the humility to admit this, and ask Jesus for assistance, He never fails.

It is by prayer that we welcome our Lord into our lives. Through prayer we gain peace of soul and joy of heart. As Jesus said, "The peace that I give, the world cannot give" (John 14:27).

We worry too much because we forget these things. We forget that Christ is ever at our side and is more anxious to aid us than we are to ask for assistance. We are frequently discouraged because we think we are alone in the world. The truth is we are never alone. Jesus is always with us, wishing to bless us with His graces.

There is the story about St. Teresa of Avila. For 18 years she was a mediocre nun in the convent. Then one day when she was 38, she walked into the chapel and looked at a picture of the suffering Christ. She had seen the picture a thousand times, but this day it suddenly seemed to come alive. It was as if she were looking at it for the first time. Seeing Jesus in agony, as though He were actually standing there, brought tears to her eyes. This experience changed her whole life.

Prior to this she had spent most of her time worrying about herself. She said that from then one she was not going to think about her illnesses. She had already spent too much time fretting about her aches and pains. She would be anxious no more; everything was in the hands of God.

Because she did this, she was able to devote her time to God. And she went out and did great things for the Lord.

Worry saps our energy. Worry takes so much of our time and strength and wears us out, and it accomplishes nothing. Worry actually can make us ill. Wouldn't it be wonderful if we all were more like St. Teresa? If we put aside our thoughts about our aches and pains and gave that time to Jesus? We too could do so much more for God.

Why don't you try it? Why not just for today give all your anxieties to Christ and let Him take care of them? You will find you are relieved of a great and useless burden, and you will discover joy. And then, free from worry, you can go out and help people in need and show them the love of Jesus.

Prayer

Please give Your blessings to families who have lost a loved one. Death is so difficult; the final parting is so very hard. Give their families strength, O Lord, to carry this cross. Give them the courage that only You can give. Help them to bear their suffering. And you, dear Blessed Mother, who stood beneath the cross and watched your dear Son die, help them, please. You know well their sorrow.

Assist, Lord, the families of the departed to realize

that parting is only for a little while. And soon, after our short life, we will be together again, happy with You, happy forever in Your beautiful and wondrous home of heaven.

God bless all those in need today: the hungry, the sick, the poor, the misunderstood, the anxious and those without faith. Take them, Lord Jesus, into Your loving arms; embrace them with Your heartfelt goodness.

Bless especially this day, Lord, those who are sick in soul. So many people are spiritually empty. They feel miserable, but they don't know why. They need You, Jesus. Please go to them and help them. Amen.

Second Week

Second Sunday of Lent

Reflection

Prayer is the most important thing you can do in this world, for in prayer you gain the blessings of Jesus, and nothing is more important than that.

It is by prayer that we revitalize our spirit by uniting ourselves with Jesus. Our Lord said, "I am the vine, you are the branches" (John 15:5). It is the vine that gives life to the branches, and without this they wither and die. It is Jesus who gives us our life and strength.

Let us remember this when we get too busy and forget to pray. As someone said, "If you are too busy to pray, you are too busy." Too many of us spend our days rushing around in circles, accomplishing little, but are busy, busy, busy — like ants on an anthill — darting and dashing in all directions all day long. Rushing about seems to be a way of life with us. But it is the way of a fool. We are spiritually blind, and we should cry out with the blind beggar in the Gospel, "Lord, that I may see" (Luke 18:41).

Many individuals try to keep up a brave front on the outside, but inside they are unhappy. They desperately need Jesus. They should take the time to pray to find Him. It is He who will give them joy and peace. Without Jesus a person can never be truly happy.

How ignorant we often are. People say they are too busy to pray, but when you talk to them for a time they can tell you every fool thing that was on television the whole past week. People should turn off the TV for 15 minutes. That alone would be healthy. But then if they spent this time in prayer, it would change their lives. People too busy to pray are only fooling themselves, and as the proverb tells us, "There is no fool like the fool who fools himself." We all have time for the things we like to do; we make time. We should make time for prayer. That is what a wise person does.

In prayer we don't have to be formal or eloquent or elegant. We don't need fancy words — only a loving, humble heart.

Prayer helps us turn away from grumbling. An individual who grumbles all the time doesn't pray very much. Prayer helps us to do less complaining. Complaining turns one into a person small in heart and narrow of mind. Prayer fills us with a graciousness and generosity and makes us big of heart and wholesome and healthy in our outlook. Hypercritical and self-centered people have hearts so shriveled up that they are too small for Jesus to enter. How sad.

Many times we feel we don't know how to pray, but that is not important. The important thing is that we try to pray, that we put ourselves into the arms of God, like a little kid running into the outstretched arms of his loving father.

Prayer

O Lord, when I feel weak and helpless, that is the time I need You the most. Please come to me. When I forget

You, please do not forget me. When I foolishly fail to pray, please overlook my failure and come to me anyway. I want You to. I want You and need You so much. I cannot begin to tell You. Never, never let me give up praying. Even when I am discouraged and there is darkness all around me, help me to continue to pray. The soul is lifeless without prayer. And I know You love me even more when I pray and do not feel like praying.

Assist me, Lord Jesus, to know that You know my needs. Don't let me waste a lot of time in prayer thinking of myself and what I do not have. Self-centered prayer is not much of a prayer at all; better than nothing, of course, but little better. You love me so much that You will accept any kind of prayer, but I long, O Lord, dearest Savior, to pray better, to think more of You and less of myself. Don't let me be telling You in prayer a lot of things You already know. Don't let me recite a long litany of my aches and pains. Just let me think of You and rest in You. Help me to realize that if I pray for others, You will take care of me. Amen.

Monday, Second Week of Lent

Reflection

It is easy to quit, to become discouraged and give up in the spiritual life. But that is the one thing a Christian cannot do. We must make our own the words of the cadet prayer at West Point, "Lord, help me to do the hard right rather than the easy wrong."

We feel sometimes in prayer that it is no use. We are

so weak and we fail; we are "vessels of clay" (2 Corinthians 4:7). But as someone has said, "The real Christian picks himself up one more time than he falls down."

We make many excuses for not praying: too busy, too tired, too this and too that. When we stop praying, however, we get our view of life all out of focus. And we lose many valuable blessings we so badly need.

The Christian in life seeks to grow in friendship with Jesus. But friendship deteriorates when we do not communicate with one another. All of us can recall close friends we had in school who are not close friends now. It is not that we like those school-day friends less; it is just that we went in different directions and failed to keep up our correspondence with them. We gradually wrote less and less, and in time we didn't write or visit at all. And so if we stop praying, visiting with Jesus, we will drift apart, not through His fault — He is always there — but through our fault. To let your friendship with Jesus deteriorate is fatal for a Christian. Then you are no longer a friend of Jesus, but a casual acquaintance, if even that.

Dr. Samuel Johnson observed that friendship is in need of constant repair. It is something that one has to work at. Friendship doesn't just happen; it must be continually renewed. Lazy people lose many friends. The lazy Christian, who has no time for prayer, who has no time for Christ, will find eventually that he is not much of a friend with Christ and he doesn't much care. That attitude spells disaster.

Jesus is always ready to visit with you. Are you willing to visit with Him? Or are you thoughtless or careless; do you always have good intentions to pray but never get around to it? Jesus is always at the door. But you have to open the door of your soul through prayer.

Prayer is vital because it daily renews our friendship with Christ. And each time we visit with Him our friendship grows. We need to pray often, and not put it off. We must pray, in the words of St. Paul, "in season and out of season" (2 Timothy 4:2), when we feel like it and when we don't feel like it. Only in that way will we keep up our friendship with Jesus. He is so sad when He sees His friends drift away. And this happens much too often. At first it is a little neglect here and there, and then it is postponing prayer, and then it is not finding time for Jesus. Finally, it is loss of close friendship with our dearest Friend.

Prayer

Dear Jesus, my dearest Friend, help me to pray when I feel least like it. I know You love me then most of all, just as a mother loves her child best when he willingly washes the dishes though he hates to. Jesus, You especially love us when we make a sacrifice to pray, just as we particularly appreciate a friend who does something for us when it is hard. If a friend drops by only when it is convenient for him, that is one thing; but when a friend comes to see us when it costs him something — that is when we are truly grateful for his friendship. Help me, Jesus, to be that kind of friend. One who will visit You in good times and bad. If I only pray when it makes me feel good — what kind of friendship is that, Lord? It is not worth very much. Friendship grows stronger in adversity. Help me, Jesus, to pray daily because that is the best way to keep our friendship alive.

Jesus, bless me. Give me the spiritual wisdom to know that if I pray often our friendship will grow, and that is what life is all about. Thank You. Amen.

Tuesday, Second Week of Lent

Reflection

Jesus is our textbook. We learn of Him, not about Him. And to know Jesus is joy. The Christ-follower frequently is at odds with the world, but he is at peace with Christ, and that is all that counts. The other way around is a tragedy. Jesus brings His love to our hearts. Cardinal Newman said, "A loveless Christian is a face too terrible to look on."

With Christ in our hearts, we are beautiful people. Perhaps we are not beautiful physically, but we are beautiful in soul and in personality. We have nothing to do with our physical makeup; this is a "given" in life. It comes from our ancestors. If you want physical beauty, you would have had to choose handsome parents. So there is not much we can do about that. But anyone can be beautiful in soul — if he tries. Anyone can have a pleasant personality — if he tries. The sadness is that anyone can do this, but many people are lazy and will not try.

The saints did precisely this, no matter what their looks were: they were people who were beautiful in soul. St. Thomas Aquinas was once asked what is necessary to be a saint and he replied simply, "Will it!" All of us can will to do something to improve ourselves in soul.

Two of the most beautiful people in our times would hardly have won a beauty contest, but they are beautiful people. Pope John XXIII and Mother Teresa of Calcutta exemplify people beautiful in the sight of God, where it really matters. Pope John had a delicious sense of humor; he once told a group of people on pilgrimage, "Wouldn't you think that if God knew from all eternity that I was going to be pope — He would have made me better-looking?'' But, in fact, good Pope John was beautiful, for his soul was alive with the love of Christ. He had a golden heart and a golden smile, so much more important than good looks, and so does Mother Teresa.

If we walk with Christ, we too can be beautiful people. Jesus will help us grow in personality. This is what He wants. Remember the parable of the talents? The men who did something with their talents were blessed; the man who did nothing was condemned (see Luke 19:11-27). Jesus wants us to do something with the talents He has given us; He wants us to improve ourselves in personality — the part of our makeup that we can do something about.

If we pray, Jesus will make us kinder, more understanding, more gentle, less angry and hostile, less critical and complaining and unpleasant. "Prayer does not change things — prayer changes us," Archbishop Fulton Sheen said. And someone else said, "If your prayers do not make you a kinder person, there is something wrong with them."

Prayer

Dear Lord, gentle Jesus, help me and bless me. Aid me to pray more and to be a better person. Help me, in the words of St. Paul, to "put on Christ" (Galatians 3:27). Prayer, I know, Lord, is not a spiritual aspirin; it is not to make me feel good. Sometimes it does, and that is fine, but that is not the real purpose of prayer. It is to make me a little more like You. The whole of Your life, dear gentle Jesus, was one of kindness. Help me to imitate You. A person doesn't have to know a lot of theology to imitate You, but one must try to be kind. One doesn't have to know a lot of Scripture to be a Christian, but he must help his neighbor.

A spiritual writer said, "If in prayer you feel you're in heaven, and yet after prayer you continue to be unkind — you had better pray a little more." Help me to understand this, dear Lord; help me to know that kindness and not piety is the first mark of Your disciples.

You will judge us, Jesus, on what we do and not what we say. There are too many Christians who are big talkers but are unkind. Do not let me be like that. Amen.

Wednesday, Second Week of Lent

Reflection

"Do not think that God loved the saints more than you," a spiritual writer wrote. Think about that. God loves each one of us so much that mere human words cannot express it. We simply stand in awe before the love that God has for us. Jesus came to earth because of this wondrous love. He gave His life for us because of His great, all-embracing love. Thomas Merton wrote, "God became man in order that man might become more like God." Isn't this a breathtaking thought? As it tells us at the Offertory of the Mass, Jesus humbled himself to participate in our humanity so that we can in some way participate in His divinity. Because of love unutterable, God lifts us up to a glory above ourselves.

The greatest mystery is not the Trinity or the Incarnation; the greatest mystery, if we reflect on it, is that God loves us and that He loves us so very, very much. And the greatest sin is to say that God, who has given us everything, does not love us. We can do a lot of things wrong, we can be very ignorant about many things, but let us never be so stupid and blind as to say God does not love us.

God loves us and, like a good father, He wants to help us, to make us better. He wants us to be more kind, more understanding and more generous. Isn't it amazing that God showers a Christian with every grace but most Christians are no better than their pagan neighbors? They foolishly ignore God's innumerable blessings.

Jesus loves us and, if we let Him, helps us to love a little more as He loves. Jesus brought to earth a message of love, and love is still the most powerful force in all the world. The love of Jesus has inspired through the centuries thousands and thousands of institutions which help people — hospitals, orphanages, homes for the elderly, soup kitchens, hospices for the poor; all open their doors to the needy in the name of Christ. Before the coming of Jesus the handicapped were despised in many places, but now, for the sake of Christ, they are embraced and loved.

Jesus did not tell us to flee the world but to bring His love into the world. He did not leave the world; just the opposite — He went to the people and lived among them. He said, "Let your light shine before men." He wished to revitalize the sick world by giving it goodness. This is the only prescription that can save the planet earth. For love brings peace, and without peace this world will blow itself up.

St. John wrote, "Anyone who says, 'I love God' and hates his brother is a liar" (1 John 4:20). Strong words, but true. He continued, "For if you do not love your neighbor, whom you see, you cannot love God, whom you do not see." But unfortunately, too many of our Christians are like this: going to church and protesting their great love for God, but at the same time being mean and unkind to their family and their neighbors. Such people are not Christians at all, no matter what they call themselves. They are hypocrites like the Pharisees, and Jesus spoke His harshest words to the Pharisees. He cannot stand hypocrisy, and He cannot stand people who call themselves Christians and yet lead unkind lives.

Prayer

Lord, spare me from hypocrisy. Let me not just talk about Christianity but live it. Christianity is not a discussion club; it is a way of life. O Lord, let me remember this. You cursed the fig tree because it looked nice but never bore any fruit. If one lives with kindness, he does not have to talk religion. Our mothers showed us what love is; they did not have to talk about it. You, Lord, cannot stomach the people who go to church but, once outside afterwards, forget everything and act in the most unkind manner; they go out of church and shut the door on You, dear Jesus, and leave You behind. And during the rest of the day and the week, at home, in business, wherever they are, they are angry, proud, and very un-Christian. Such people, and they are many, are the worst advertisement there is for Christianity. Please, Lord, let me not be this way; let me learn from You and imitate You. Let me realize that to truly follow You I must this day show a little of Your kindness. Amen.

Thursday, Second Week of Lent

Reflection

God wants us to be happy; why then are we so downcast? Because we are lacking in faith. St. Francis of Assisi lived in far worse times than ours, and he was among the happiest people who ever lived, for he had a strong faith that God would take care of things. We worry too much because of our weak faith. We look at the world and see so much trouble it upsets us, and we think we humans have to solve every problem. Where is our faith? This is God's world, and He knows what to do and how to handle things. We should pray, and leave everything in the hands of God. St. Francis de Sales said, "God will make possible what seems impossible to us."

A Christian should not worry all the time like a pagan who has no faith. If we look and talk as gloomy as our neighbors without religion, we are not going to attract people to Christ. The reason so many wanted to follow St. Francis of Assisi is not that he was a great orator or a brilliant thinker, for he was neither; they followed him because he was so happy, and they wanted to know what made him happy. Would people today follow you because you are such a happy Christian? Or have you become a pessimist like your neighbors without religion? Are you converting others to Christ by your Christian joy; or have you been converted to pagan pessimism by your irreligious neighbors?

St. Paul said, "Rejoice in the Lord always; again, I say, Rejoice!" (Philippians 4:4). Do you follow this injunction of Paul? If a Christian cannot be happy, then who in this whole wide world can be?

Our Creator made us for happiness. After all, our final destiny is heaven, and that is a place of perfect happiness. If we are heaven-bound we should have joy in our hearts. Teilhard de Chardin said, "Joy is the infallible sign of the presence of God."

Puritanical people have turned the beautiful, happy message of Christianity upside-down. That is what happens when humans tamper with the divine teachings. Puritanical people tell us that religion must be sad and gloomy; they do not walk around with happy hearts like St. Francis of Assisi; they walk around with long, sour faces, in a funereal atmosphere. Their philosophy seems to be, "If it is fun, it must be a sin; if it is beautiful, tear it down." How far such individuals have departed from the religion of Jesus. When people wander away from Christ and His Church and make up their own religion, no matter how well-intentioned, they end in disaster. They make a travesty of true Christianity.

Real Christians are like St. Teresa of Avila, who prayed, "O Lord, from sour-faced saints and silly devotions, deliver me." Saints show us the way. Because they prayed, God blessed them with common sense and a sense of humor. It never entered their minds to leave the Church and start another. That to them would have been utter folly. One does not desert a Christ-made faith for one made by man.

Prayer

Dear Jesus, teach me to be joyful of heart. A religion of doom and bleakness is a perversion of what You taught us. Such a religion turns people off. Help them to see that this is not true Christianity. With You, dear Jesus, there is happiness. Many in our country who rebel against religion are revolting against the gloom of puritanical people, not the joy of Your faith, Jesus. Give them the wisdom to make the distinction; give them the guidance to find You and the happiness of real Christianity. Puritanical people make a mockery of the true faith, for Your message, Lord, was the "good news." The crowds rejoiced when they heard what You said. You brought happiness to a world awash in the gloom of paganism. You taught love and joy, Lord; let people see that those who try to make Your religion something drab and bleak are leading us away from You and not to You. Help me, by my happiness and kindness, to show You, dear Jesus, to others. Amen.

Friday, Second Week of Lent

Reflection

When God created the world, He looked upon it and said, "It is good" (see Genesis 1:10ff). Man is good, though he is weak and sometimes fails. But God gave us life because He loves us, each one of us. He made us for happiness — that is our heart's desire. If God did not want us to be happy, why did He make this wish the deepest desire within us? This is the way we were made. We should be no more ashamed of the fact that we want to be happy than a zebra should be ashamed that he has black and white stripes. God made both of us to be that way.

All things are good. God cannot create anything evil. It is only when we misuse things or abuse them that evil happens. We were made by God for goodness and happiness. The sad thing is that many people are looking for happiness in places where they will never find it. It is only God who can give us happiness. He made us, and He alone can make us happy, for He is the source and giver of all joy.

For example, if a person was in a room that was cold and there was a fire in the fireplace, the closer he came to the fire the warmer he would be, for fire is the source and giver of heat. God is the source and giver of happiness. So the closer we come to Him the happier we will be. Unfortunately, many people seemingly do not believe this or realize it. For there are many unhappy people. Archbishop Fulton Sheen said, "Never in the history of the world have there been more unhappy people than there are today."

People disregard God and then wonder why they are miserable. As Shakespeare said, "What fools these mortals be." Some seek happiness in pleasure or popularity or power or possessions. But these can never make one happy. Still proud people, who will not listen to reason, pursue them. Like stubborn little kids, they insist on doing everything their way, and they get deeper and deeper into the swamp. They are victims of their own folly. They end up ruining their lives, and hurting many others. One could only wish that they wake up before disaster hits.

It would be different if we had more than one life to live. Then wasting one wouldn't be so foolish. But the fact is that we have but one life. Throwing it away through pride is a catastrophe. Pursuing happiness down dead-end streets, even though we have traveled that way before to no avail, does not seem like what a wise man would do. Pleasure, money, popularity turn to ashes in our mouth, and yet many go out and try the same thing over again. If these things brought happiness, then Hollywood stars should be the happiest people in the world. But are they? All their divorces, all their running to psychiatrists, all their suicides and attempted suicides hardly sound like happiness to me. Must we be hit on the head before we wake up?

Prayer

Dear Lord, the proverb says, "Pride goes before the fall" (see Proverbs 16:18). Help me to overcome my pride. Why must I be so stubborn, like a spoiled child? I know You are the way, but I am headstrong, and I want to go my own way, which is the cause of so much of my troubles. Give me good sense, Lord. Give me a little wisdom, so I will be guided by You. St. Augustine said, "There are three things necessary for learning. The first is humility, the second is humility, the third is humility." Help me to be humble, so I will learn, so I will walk in Your ways. You said to the Apostles, "Come, follow me" (Matthew 2:20). You say this same thing to me. Help me to respond the way the Apostles did: "they left all and followed him" (Luke 5:11). Put away my pride. So often it is the people with the least talent who are the most proud. The gifted people are humble because they know how much they depend upon You, Lord. Bless me so that I will be more like them.

Bless too my loved ones, my relatives and friends. Bless especially those who have gone before us in death. We loved them in this life, and our prayers go with them. When we pray for them we continue to show we love them. Amen.

Saturday, Second Week of Lent

Reflection

We find ourselves in God. We find our self-realization in being like God, for, the Bible tells us, we are made to His likeness. God is Love, so we must love.

The discovery of ourselves in God gives us the light to see that we must be people who love. We exist because of God's love, and we must pass on that love. We share in God's love, and we must let others share in our love.

We become ourselves when we become most like God and give away our love; indeed the best way to love ourselves is to love others. In reaching out to embrace others, we are most like God. The more love I keep for myself, the less love I have.

Our greatest gift, the gift of life, is a gift of love from God. The quality of our lives depends on our being God-like and giving the gift of ourselves to others. If we are not lazy and are willing to put forth the effort, we will use the talent God has given us and find fulfillment.

Many people think they are too sophisticated today for religion; they tell us that religion is too old-fashioned for modern man. They do not realize that truth is eternal, especially the truths of Christ, and never old-fashioned. Christ is the same, yesterday, today and forever. Fashion has nothing to do with Him or what He told us. Our modern sophisticated people are a bit mixed-up, and in the end, since they are not wise enough amid all their so-called knowledge, to find their way out of the closet, they end up in despair. They are not intelligent enough to know the truth and are too proud to look for it. They unfortunately follow the philosophy of pessimism of the irreligious popular writers of our day, and do not follow the great and wise men of all ages who were men of religion. They are too prone to welcome everybody else's popular but wrong solutions, the fashionable "thinking" of the moment. They give in to their natural lazy impulses and accept easy answers. They are like sheep who blindly follow any current notion that circulates in the flock.

But God expects us to think. As the ancient Athenian philosophers said, "Let reason rule." God gave us intelligence so that we might use it and think for ourselves — not play "follow the leader" in the world of ideas. It is sad that we live in such a comfort-loving society that many will not think because it is difficult. So they let others, self-appointed "experts," do their thinking for them — while they pursue pleasure — and only wake up too late and find that these "experts" have led them and lost them. It is sad that so many people today follow "thinkers" who are even more bewildered than they are, "the blind leading the blind." In our world, in our times, we must realize that silly solutions have currency and we are silly to follow them. And we must learn that just because a writer is bold and articulate, that does not make him wise.

Prayer

Lord Jesus, help me to know that You and You alone have true wisdom. The wise of this world are often fools, and we are foolish to follow them. We will forever be unhappy if we do not let You be our guide. A person tortured by his egotism and pride who chooses himself for a guide is the most foolish of all. O dear Jesus, I am often an unthinking individual; give me Your light. I need most of all Your wise words. Let me not be deceived by false prophets, just because they are flashy and modern. Let me listen to You, Lord; let me prayerfully attend to Your words of wisdom in the Gospel. You have told us that we must love and help one another. Therein we find fulfillment; a happiness that is sought for ourselves alone will never be found. Only by being a giving person will I know joy. Amen.

Third Week

Third Sunday of Lent

Reflection

Jesus taught us that mankind is a family, and we must look after one another. We are to give others our love. Actually love is the only gift that we have to give away — everything else has been given to us — and we should be generous in giving it. The love that we have given will be the most important thing that we did in life when we stand before the Lord in judgment. We have numerous opportunities to share our love, visiting or calling the sick and shut-ins, smiling at others we meet, complimenting those who have done worthwhile things, not complaining when we would like to, and not answering anger with anger.

One woman says that she writes a note of good cheer to someone every day. We all love to receive happy letters; why not send a few? Some individuals write letters but only tell of bad things; they could be called "Calamity Jane" because all they speak of is calamity. We know enough of unpleasant things; how beautiful when, like this woman, we pass over the gloom and write about the beautiful things. We can't afford to send flowers, but we can send notes that, like flowers, are full of joy. Someone told this lady that to send out a pleasant note each day was expensive. She replied, "Well, I don't smoke. If I were buying cigarettes I would be spending a lot of money. Now I spend that money on stamps to cheer people up." And Jesus loves her for her generosity. We could do the same.

The woman did not buy expensive stationery, just plain white. She knew people don't care as much about the writing paper as what is written on it. Sometimes she buys or cuts out little pictures and sticks them in the corner, and sometimes she just draws a happy little clown face with a big, bright smile.

As Christians, we don't have to do big things. Did the Blessed Mother do big things? But Jesus wants us to do something. He wants us to contribute to the love and happiness that this old world so badly needs.

As Christians we little people don't have to do great penances. Let our penance be a smile, especially when we don't feel like smiling. Let our penance be talking about something pleasant and not about all our illnesses.

There are so many gloomy people around. Can they be followers of Jesus, who came from heaven to bring us joy? Jesus rose from the dead. He was victorious over evil and sin. Let us rejoice with Him and pass on His great joy.

Prayer

Lord Jesus, the highlight of Christianity is Easter, for You rose from the dead. We say, "Happy Easter," and so it is. Christianity is not the bad news, but the "good news." Let me spread good news, O Jesus. Those who go about morose and dejected do not know You, Lord, very well. We are not pagans who have no hope; they indeed have a right to be morbid and bitter. For them life is not worth living. But this is not the philosophy of the Christian. God gave us life; God sustains our life. God sent You, Lord, to come to earth to save us from sin and from gloom. You came to us with Your blessings and happiness. How great Your gifts are to us. Should we Christians then sit around pouting like a spoiled child at Christmas with a room full of presents?

Thank You, Jesus, for coming to us. Thank You for remaining with us, even after You returned to heaven. Thank You for Your innumerable graces. Lord, we look to You for help, and Your help is always there. Thank You. We know we do not have to journey alone. Thank You, Lord. Amen.

Monday, Third Week of Lent

Reflection

We should pray so that we may be an instrument in God's providence. As God's instrument we love others with His love. As God's instrument, we abandon ourselves into His hands and let Him guide us and help us do His work in the world. Only the strong, sure love of God can give us the strength and clear-sightedness to be Christ-like in our efforts.

When in the Our Father we pray, "Thy kingdom come," we are asking that God's love may fill the world. And we should also ask Him that we may be privileged to help Him in this great and wonderful work.

There is a story of a GI in Italy during World War II. The fighting was fierce, and his outfit was in the middle of it for many hours. Finally, he and his company moved into a village and were given a short rest. He was so tired he dropped in his tracks and fell asleep. When he awoke he looked around; he had been sleeping on the steps of a bombed-out church. He got up and went in. There he saw that everything was destroyed except a statue of the Sacred Heart up in the front. He moved closer and noticed that though the statue was intact, the hands had been blown off. Still closer, he saw a small sign scratched on cardboard at the foot of the statue, put there by another GI, and the sign said, "I have no hands but yours." In truth, we are the hands and the love of God in the world today; Jesus needs us to help people with our hands to do as He did when He walked on earth.

The more I help others, the more Christ-like I am. The less I help others, the less of a person I become, for selfishness shrivels and shrinks the soul. It is for us then to love one another in Christ. God loves every soul born into the world. We are here to help Him show that love.

If we pass on the love of Jesus, we will be happy. The trouble with life is that these days too many people are always saying, "What's in it for me?"

Remember the parable our Lord told about the king who gave the banquet? Many could not come because they desired things for themselves. They did not have time to share their love at the banquet. They did not know that if they had sacrificed and gone to the banquet the king would have provided for all their needs in life. The king in the story, of course, is God. As Jesus said, "Seek you first the kingdom of God and everything else will be given to you" (see Matthew 6:33, Luke 12:31).

There was great joy among the early Christians. The pagans said, "See the Christians — see how they love one another." Would people be able to say that of us Christians today? Is it our selfishness and lack of giving love that is at heart the reason for our unhappiness? A person who loves himself too much hurts himself. When we want too many possessions, we make ourselves discontent. When we own too many possessions, they end up owning us.

Prayer

Dear Lord, here I am. I am not going to tell You all about my aches and pains. You know these things already. I am not going to spend my precious time with You talking about my troubles. I just ask You to give me strength for today. Help me to carry on, to be pleasant, to try to help someone in need and not to think so much about myself. You did not give me life to be selfish, self-seeking and self-centered. You gave me life to show others Your unfailing love. Help me to do this today.

Let me call a lonely shut-in today and say cheerful things, or visit a sick person and tell him I am praying for him and thinking about him. Just help me to do something for someone else. My trouble is I spend too much time thinking about myself, and then I get bogged down in self-pity. It is easy to do — and so useless. Let me look on this day as an opportunity to help another, so I will have a little jewel in my heavenly crown. True, my health is not all that good and I have family worries (what family hasn't?) and I am anxious about many things — well, dear Jesus, I am not going to think about these things today. I am going to forget them by helping someone else. Amen.

Tuesday, Third Week of Lent

Reflection

The Christ-follower hopes in God, whom he does not see, trusts in God to bring him to the possession of things that are beyond imagination.

By faith we know God, without seeing Him; by hope we possess God, without feeling His presence, but we have confidence in Him even in our darkness. By love we become like God, sharing His goodness. That is why St. Paul said, "We have these three, faith, hope and love, but the greatest of these is love" (1 Corinthians 13:13).

Because the candle of our faith, hope and love burns so dimly, religion is so often ignored by many in the world. They see that it seems to do so little for us Christians that they conclude it must be worthless. But it is not Christianity that is at fault, it is half-hearted Christians. Because we have so many Christians who are Christ-followers in name but not in deed, religion in our day is disregarded and ridiculed. People look at so many half-hearted Christians, who are no better than their irreligious neighbors, and they say, "If that is all Christianity does for a person, I want no part of it."

A real Christian shows the love of Jesus. A true Christian gives away that love. As the song tells us,

"Love in your heart wasn't put there to stay,
love isn't love 'til you give it away."

Let us pray that Christ will help us to be more loving — and more cheerful. We are told that the first curse God visits on those who are unfaithful to Him is to take away their sense of humor. Help me, Lord, to laugh more, and especially to laugh at myself. Never let me take myself too seriously. We already have too many serious and somber Christians. Why must I go around anxious and fretting, if I believe and hope in You? That doesn't make sense. I should be — if my faith is real — as cheerful and carefree as a child. Jesus said, "Unless you become as little children, you shall not enter the kingdom of heaven" (Matthew 18:3). Help me to be like that, Lord. If I had real faith I would say, "This is God's world. He can take care of things, and He can take care of me." If I thought like that I would be happy. Certainly St. Francis of Assisi was happy, and the world then was much worse than it is today. He did not waste time worrying. He rolled up his sleeves and went to work to make things better. We have too many people who wring their hands about the trouble in the world — and do nothing. The saints did something, no matter how small. Bigness is not important to Jesus, but doing something is very important.

There is a story told about good Pope John XXIII. He would say his night prayers and remember so many great problems that he had to deal with, but at the end he would smile and say, "Dear God, it's Your Church — I'm going to bed."

Prayer

Lord, let me leave the great problems of the world in Your hands. Does a child worry, or does he go about carefree because he knows his father will take care of things? Shouldn't we have this same faith in our heavenly Father?

Help me to have the faith and humor of good Pope John. Help me to be humble enough to know that if anything worthwhile is to be done — God must do it. As the sentence in the psalms tells us, "Unless the Lord build the house, they labor in vain who build it" (Psalm 127:1).

Laughter goes with love. Laughing with others and laughing at myself sets me free from the prison and pride and the tyranny of pettiness. With laughter and love we are fully alive.

If I am sincere in my prayers, then I will not worry. For in my prayers I tell God I trust Him, I put all things in His hands, and I know that like a loving Father He will take care of everything. Amen.

Wednesday, Third Week of Lent

Reflection

Too many people go to seed too early in life. They let their minds go to sleep; their souls are dormant. They pray little, or so routinely it is hardly prayer at all. Their lives are dull, one dreary day after another. Such an individual might as well be a cabbage.

Why do people get into such a state? Perhaps it is because they get too comfortable and lazy. In the Old Testament in Isaiah, God is angry at an unfaithful country and He says boldly, "Make the heart of this people fat!" (Isaiah 6:10). He did this, of course, as a punishment. A rich, comfortable, fat people destroy themselves. Is this what is happening in our land? We have such a drive for riches, the very thing that in the long run can do many people the most harm. For "the love of money is the root of all evils" (1 Timothy 6:10). Not that money in itself is harmful, but it is too easy to misuse. Prosperity is harder to handle than poverty. Yet everyone wants to get rich. With some people it is a great blessing from God that they are not rich — for wealth would ruin them.

We must wake up and view life more from God's point of view. Wealth and riches are not the end of life for the Christian; that is what the greedy, base-minded people seek. And they end up very unhappy. Happiness is more important than wealth; indeed, rich people are most often unhappy, for they are forever worried about losing their money.

True happiness is living with Jesus; then life is full of goodness and beauty, and one's heart is radiant and aglow. With Jesus a person can achieve wonderful things, for Jesus works with us and through us.

Too many Christians are too much like their non-religious neighbors. Like these neopagans who live all around us, many Christians seek riches, comfort, pleasure, instead of Christ. They are, like their neighbors, in a rut of always criticizing and complaining. We are supposed to be happy with the joy of Jesus, yet we act like those who have no religion and are wretched. Certainly continual complaining is a sign of unhappiness; constant criticism means one is not at peace.

The constant critic actually is a peculiar person. He never does anything himself, he just waits and sits around until someone else does something, and then he speaks out — against it. He is against everything. He lets others do the work, and then he says it is all wrong. The critic, a hopeless, unhappy creature, has only one purpose in life: he tries to tear down everything the builders try to put up. A political figure once was asked about his critics, and he responded, "Every dog must have a few fleas."

The continual critic is a pessimist. Looking at a glass with water half way up, the optimist says, "It's half full," but the pessimist says, "It's half empty." On a bright and beautiful sunny day, he only sees the shadows and dwells on them. In a doughnut shop there was a sign that said, "As you go through life — keep this ever as your goal — keep your eye upon the doughnut — and not upon the hole."

Prayer

Lord, don't let me be a complainer. Don't let me be like those who are always thinking and talking about what they don't have instead of about what they do. Let me have a grateful heart. Let me count my blessings.

The complainer spends his whole day making himself unhappy. But a disciple of Yours, dear Jesus, cannot be a pessimist. You rose from the dead, and in that Easter victory You have given us hope. So a pessimistic and unhopeful Christian is a contradiction in terms.

Let me live close to You, Lord, so Your hope and love will be with me. The flame of Your love, Jesus, makes us new. Without You, O Christ, evil would flood the world and we would be plunged into deepest darkness and we would have reason indeed to despair. But we have You, Jesus, and Cardinal Newman said, "God gives us strength according to our day." You help us; You give us what we need for each day. Monsignor Ronald Knox wrote that He who got us this far in life can surely take us the rest of the way. Amen.

Thursday, Third Week of Lent

Reflection

Jesus wants our love and friendship more than anything else. He wants to have us visit Him in prayer. He waits for us. Sometimes we are halfhearted; we feel a dryness of soul; the words won't come. But Jesus does not care about beautiful words or whether in prayer we are having a "religious high." He is our Friend and with a friend one does not always have to be gabbing. If words will not come, if we are unable to think of spiritual things, then we can just sit there with our Friend, quietly giving Jesus our time. That is prayer too.

Karl Rahner wrote, "Unless we pray we do not truly know Christ, and our religion is reduced to a purely human fellow-feeling." But such a "good-feeling" religion does not last, for whenever we feel bad we give up. Genuine Christianity is, above all, perseverance, loyal and true to the end. Without prayer one will be a "dropout" when things get difficult. Is that any way to treat our Friend? Without prayer we get tired of being kind and unselfish; we get bored with doing good. Without prayer a person cuts off his spiritual plant at the roots, and it withers and dies.

We need Jesus, for He can untie things that are now knotted in our lives and He can tie up things that are dangling loose. So in prayer we turn to Him. C.S. Lewis wrote, "What fools we are if we think we do not need God's help. We are all beggars before God." When we are humble enough to fully realize this, we are starting to grow in the spiritual life. Humility is the beginning. Henri Gheon wrote a book entitled *The Secret of the Saints*. The "secret," the one thing that all the saints had in order to grow in love, no matter what country, no matter whether rich or poor, was humility. All the saints had humility, and because of this they asked God to help them and He did. That is why they were saints. When are we going to ask God to help us to be humble?

We are all like little kids who can just barely crawl. The secret of the saints is that in their humility they called out to God to help them and He came to them and picked them up and carried them along. The saints were no different from us in many ways, but they put aside their petty pride and humbly begged the Lord for help. That is why they became wonderful instruments for God in the world.

We may never be able to do big things, but God also expects us to be His instruments for good while we are here on earth. In the words of the old hymn, we are to "brighten the corner where you are." As Confucius said, "Better to light one candle than to curse the darkness." Let us humbly petition God for the grace to do this.

Prayer

Lord, too many today want someone else to do the work. But You want us to do it. They are always saying, "Why doesn't the government do this? Why doesn't the bishop do that?" It is always someone else.

There is a priest who works with poor people in the slums, and he said this: "When I first started here, if the street was dirty, I called city hall. And often nothing was done, and I became angry. Now when I see the street is dirty, I get a broom and sweep it."

You want us to work, to do things to make our little

part of the world better. If we wait for others to do it, we will wait forever. It doesn't make any difference if what we do is not big and important. You will not judge by results but by efforts. If I sit around and complain because others are not doing big things, and I do next to nothing myself — I'm going to have a lot of explaining to do to You on judgment day.

Also, if I only pray for myself and my loved ones — that is not enough. I pray then, Lord, for all the poor souls in purgatory. Many who were so good to us in this life have gone before us in death. Now is our opportunity to do something for them. Bless them, Jesus, help them, shower them with Your holy graces. Bless all those in need of prayers. Amen.

Friday, Third Week of Lent

Reflection

Our spiritual strength and inner courage fail us entirely if we do not pray. Without prayer, sooner or later a person falls apart. It is prayer then that aids us to overcome our fears and makes our failures bearable. Jesus helps to calm us down when we get too nervous and "hyper." Jesus helps us to be more patient and less irritable, less resentful and revengeful. He helps us to better bear criticism about us. He assists us in getting rid of our false values; He takes the anger out of our hearts and pulls up the weeds of vice in the garden of our soul, replacing them with the beautiful flowers of kindness. For Jesus is our sunshine.

To overcome faults is frequently painful; that is why we need Christ to be there to aid us. If we pray, then He "leads us to see new paths and hear new melodies." He lifts our hearts above sin and worry, lifts them up to the beauty of God.

Prayer opens our eyes and ears to Jesus. Whatever we say, no matter how feeble our prayers may be, pleases Him. We only have to pray and Jesus blesses us and our loved ones and all in need.

One of the reasons some people do not pray is that they are afraid of silence. We live in such a noisy world that we get nervous when the noise stops. But we need a quiet time and a quiet place to pray. The Trappist monks say, "Silence is the language of God." God cannot get our attention amid noise and busy surroundings. We have to go aside, "far from the madding crowd." We have to take time out from our busyness to give a rest to our soul and let the Lord refresh it. A weary soul, like a tired body, can do little.

Let us go aside to be with Jesus. Let us "sit right down and have a little talk with the Lord." Prayer feeds our hungry souls. Prayer puts the disjointed parts of life back together again. Prayer orients us, reminding us once more of the true purpose of human existence. It is so easy to lose one's way in our chaotic, bewildering world. We need, then, time for silence and time for prayer, so we can recapture the meaning of life and return afresh to our duties.

Prayer makes us more gentle, more humble. If we are to be true to Christ we must be continually, day by day, little by little, striving to be kinder people. When we are united with Jesus in the precious moments of prayer, we grow in grace. And with Jesus we have the strength to show others the love of the Lord.

You alone, O Lord, can give to humans what they are searching for.

Prayer

Dearest Jesus, dearest Friend, Savior and Lord, why is my heart so cold and my soul so spiritless? Warm me with the glowing goodness of Your Sacred Heart. When the disciples were on the way to Emmaus, You talked to them, but they did not recognize You. But then afterwards they did, and they chastised themselves saying, "Surely we should have known who he was, for when he talked to us of the Scriptures, our hearts were on fire" (see Luke 24:32). Please kindle my lukewarm heart, as You did the hearts of the disciples. Refresh my soul and set my heart on fire; let the burning love with which You love the world, dear Christ, fill my soul. You want to renew the world, O Lord, but first of all we, Your followers, must be renewed in heart. Please help us. You must give us the grace or we cannot do Your work. My soul is small and weak; assist me, Jesus, so that I will think and act more like You.

I am trying, Lord, I am trying. St. Paul said, "Let this mind be in you which was also in Christ" (Philippians 2:5). I pray for this. If I think the way You thought, then, like You, I will show goodness and comfort to others. Amen.

Saturday, Third Week of Lent

Reflection

Success is "not being defeated by failure." This is especially true in the spiritual life. To succeed spiritually a person must put his trust in Jesus. We must have faith. We need to pray in the words of the man with the sick son: "I believe; help my unbelief" (Mark 9:24).

Recall that Jesus would not work a miracle unless the individual had faith. At Capernaum when the friends of the paralyzed man let him down on the stretcher through the opening in the roof to the feet of Christ, Jesus looked at him and saw the faith in his eyes and then cured him. He perceived such faith that He healed him both in body and in soul; He took away his physical infirmity and also his sins (see Luke 5:18-25).

When the cloak of Jesus was touched by the sick woman, Jesus said, "Daughter, your faith has made you whole" (Luke 8:48). When Christ touched the eyes of the blind man he said, "According to your faith, let it be done to you" (Matthew 9:29).

St. Paul's disciples said, "Without faith it is impossible to please God" (Hebrews 11:6), and added, "My just man lives by faith" (10:38). When faith dries up, the plant of our devotion and good deeds dies. We must pray then to grow in faith. Too many of us can say, "I am lazy, Lord, and, as a result, I postpone prayer, and I am so ordinary in my devotion to You." And as someone wrote, "Mediocrity can be a terrible form of tyranny." When we love our comfort, when we are complacent and content with being average — it is such a waste.

The fact is that often in our daily clack-clack life we don't feel much like praying. Prayer is frequently irksome, and any excuse to omit it is welcomed. But that is the very time that we must pray and persevere in prayer. The saints tell us, "To attain the final goal one must endure." Satan tries in every way to discourage us; he tells us especially when we are downhearted that it is useless. There are indeed many days when we feel powerless against the avalanche of folly and crime in the world and we want then to give up. But it is precisely then that we need to pray even more. In these dark times we must look to the crucifix and see Jesus in His darkest hour and how He yet endured this agony and heartache because He loves us so very, very much. As Cardinal Newman said, "How great is the mercy of God for us, how wondrous His compassion, how inscrutable is God's love for us sinners." The Lord is gracious and kind. He loves us even unto death. We cannot forget that; we cannot fail Him who loves us so graciously and so generously.

We must remember that it is prayer that makes our deeds worthwhile; it is prayer that supplies the spiritual fuel for our souls so that we can help our neighbors in need. We must then continue to pray for the sake of Jesus; we must never give up.

Prayer

Lord Jesus, I pray for my family and friends, living and dead. Take care of them. Bless our home and all homes. Shower Your graces on all who are in need. Help those who will die today. Help those who have suffered a tragedy. Help those who do not think of You, for they are the ones who need You the most.

Walk beside us today. Assist those who are despairing to get up and pick up the pieces and try again.

Dear Blessed Mother, I entrust my loved ones especially to your care. You are a mother and you know how to look after little ones. Cast your special look of love on all children, especially on those who are ill and mistreated and hungry and those who are not loved.

Dear Mary, protect all of us, for all of us are your children. Jesus on the cross gave you to us to be our Mother. We look to you; we ask for your motherly love and care this day. Amen.

Fourth Week

Fourth Sunday of Lent

Reflection

Rose Kennedy in our own day has been an example of Christian courage. She always went to daily Mass. She knew many sorrows, and yet she would not let tragedy conquer her. After the assassination of her two sons, she said, "I will not be vanquished by these events." She said that too many people depended on her and she would not let them down. She, who so often had welcomed Christ into her heart in Holy Communion, had in her crises the courage of Christ.

God gives courage to us also, if we turn to Him. We live in an anxious age; our society is jittery and nervous. Everyone seems to be taking pills for this and that. What we all need is more confidence in God. Indeed without God we are failures even when we succeed.

We live in a prosperous country, but even affluent people appear these days deeply discouraged. We live in a nation that is the garden spot of the world, and still amid all this so many seem unhappy. Is it because most people neglect God?

It is God who gives us strength and it is God who gives us happiness. Surely we Christians must know this. A

Christian should not be paralyzed by pessimism. We know that Christ can accomplish amazing things, and that if we work together with Christ we can be an unbeatable team.

A Christian cannot have a tragic view of life, like those who are unbelieving. We know that God runs the world; our secret weapon is hope.

To be sure, man alone can do little, but man is not alone. Those without faith may think so and therefore stumble along in life. Often these people are the most proud. As Dr. Samuel Johnson said of one man, "He was dull in a new way, and that made many think him important." Some today feel that their philosophy of doom and gloom makes them important.

How can a human alone think he is great and strut around on the stage of life like a peacock? The greatest mind is but a tiny grain of sand compared to God, who is like the mighty, majestic ocean. Pride deludes people.

It was the saints who in their humility were truly important, because they gave their lives entirely over to God to use as He wished. "Be it done unto me according to thy word," the Blessed Mother said (Luke 1:38), and she is a model for all the other saints. When one does this he is a new being, and man with God is truly important. The saints walked with God and moved mountains. They did more than anyone. Because they looked to God and gave themselves to God, body and soul, because God was with them to help them every step of the way, they accomplished truly great things on earth.

Prayer

Bless our country, O Lord. America needs our prayers. It is a good and gracious nation, and we are thankful for it, but it has many problems like all countries. Enlighten our leaders, our President and Congress and our judges. Guide them in making the right decisions. Give them wisdom, and may they always act justly. Grant our nation peace in our times and for all times. We have had too much war. War is so terrible; help us always to live in peace.

We ask You to bless the brave men who gave their lives that we might enjoy freedom. This is one of our greatest gifts, and it has been purchased by a great deal of "blood, sweat and tears." Many have lost their lives so that we can live as free people. We are grateful for our liberty.

Bless our farmers, who provide us with food, and our workers, who make the things that we need and enjoy. We have so many good things in this country, more than most other people in the world. Thank You, Lord, thank You for being so kind to us. Bless all in our country who serve and help the people. Amen.

Monday, Fourth Week of Lent

Reflection

Jesus has the answers in life. We turn to Him and follow Him, if we are wise. Existence without our Lord is an exercise in futility. People who follow mere human pundits in the ever-changing fads and fancies of the moment are walking down the wrong road.

Jesus is our salvation. Following Him is more difficult than following the worldly philosophy, but it is all worth it and more. The worldly way is to continue to play, long after we have left childhood; Jesus, on the other hand, asks us to climb the mountain with Him, but what an exhilarating experience that is. Playing all the time as an adult leaves us jaded, bored, empty. Life with Jesus leaves us fulfilled.

We must not just follow the crowd in life. We must not be swept off our feet by the current popular opinion, so often wrong. We must not do things simply because "everyone is doing it." That frequently is the very reason not to do it. Someone has said that we are "a nation of sheep." We are so afraid to be different; we are such conformists. And unfortunately the trend-setters in our society are often empty-headed people. Any addlebrained individual who is clever, bold and articulate can call himself a leader and get publicity to set a new style. Then TV, our brainless picture toy, picks up his senseless new notion and tries to brainwash the public with it. This is done, for instance, in the world of clothing styles. One simply cannot be caught dead, we are told over and over again, wearing last year's fashions. We must throw out all those good clothes in our closets and buy the "latest" styles. The cardinal sin is wearing clothes that someone in New York or Paris has arbitrarily said are no longer "in." And we, the public, jump through their hoop and buy all the things they tell us to — while they "laugh all the way to the bank." How smart are we?

All this is pretty foolish in the world of clothing, but the same process is attempted also in the world of books and ideas. We are constantly being bombarded with the best-seller list. We are told we must buy these books to keep up with society. We are informed that it is a sacrilege not to buy every foolish new book that many other fools have bought. We are all supposed to think alike — and the thinking of the modern book world is often pagan. But, "they say" — whoever "they" are — that we must think in the popular fashion about morality, for instance, or we will be ridiculed for being old-fashioned. And usually the current fashion in morality is "anything goes." Hollywood sets the trend, but most Hollywood stars don't have a brain in their heads. Most often, we should be doing just the opposite of Hollywood, if we want to be true to ourselves and true to Jesus.

Prayer

Lord, don't let me be a follower when it means going against what You taught. Don't let me follow TV religion, which is often the easy way; TV religious leaders are frequently entertainers and masters of emotional showmanship rather than people of thoughtful spirituality. Christianity is not a religion to make us feel good. We should be the last to follow the popular, half-educated, so-called leaders of our society, and the first to follow You, O Lord. Christianity is not the easy way. Nothing worthwhile in life is easy. John Gardner wrote a book entitled *No Easy Victories*. That is what You taught, dear Jesus. Counterfeit "thinkers" give us a kind of short-cut way of life, but it is, in the end, hollow and empty, and not real religion at all. Help me to see this, Lord. Help me not to be fooled by the fast talkers who are false guides, but to follow You who are my true Leader. Don't let me be misled in life, Lord. Amen.

Tuesday, Fourth Week of Lent

Reflection

After the Ascension the angel said to the Apostles, "Why do you stand here looking up in the sky?" (Acts 1:11). The Christ-follower is not supposed to be a stargazer, a daydreamer. We are supposed to be active and apostolic. We are supposed to look around and see people in need (not like the priest who passed by the man dying in the ditch with unseeing eyes in the parable of the Good Samaritan). We are supposed to help others.

What a person does needn't be earth-shaking. The important thing is to do something. We can help others break the tension of modern living by our kindness — before the tension breaks them. The Christian is a realist and knows that things will not get better just by wishing. We have to make them better. And we can do this by daily acts of kindness. This is the Christian way to change the world. We don't need big million-dollar projects and endless committee meetings; what we need is for each Christ-follower to be more kind to his family and to improve his neighborhood.

We little people cannot cure all the problems of the world, but we can make the block we live on a better place and our home a more loving shelter for our family.

A house where there is no love is just a house, and no amount of decorating and beautiful furniture can make it otherwise. The most expensive house with the most wonderful rooms is empty unless it is filled with love. It takes a lot of love to make a house a home. It is something a family, and every member of the family, must work at every day. Money can only buy a house; it can never buy a home. If a person gives his house everything but love, he has given it nothing. If the members of a family give their home love, they will find that it needs little else.

Some families neglect common courtesy in the home, but it should be practiced there more than anywhere. "Charity begins at home." An effort at a little more kindness would go a long way to make your home happier. Some people are so courteous out in public, at business or at a party, but when they come home they act like a bear. This will never do for a Christian. The people you love the most are in your home, and you must show them love. If you want to be cranky, then act that way somewhere else — but not at home. It is easy at home to forget to say "please" and "thank you." But this is a mistake. Courtesy is needed there more than anywhere. Courtesy reduces family friction and keeps things running smoothly; courtesy is like oil for a machine. When we are thoughtful and kind we contribute to the love in our home. When we are gentle and peacemakers we help put out the fires of anger and antipathy that can arise where people live in close contact with one another.

Some people wonder what they can do for Christ. Begin by increasing the love in your own home. Start by smiling more and saying "please" and "thank you" to your own family.

Prayer

Dear Lord, today I pray for the poor souls in purgatory. We know that in praying for them we can help them, and that they will pray for us. One of the most beautiful teachings of the Church is the Communion of Saints.

We are not alone in our struggles in life; we are never alone. The saints and our loved ones in heaven are praying for us, and the souls in purgatory pray for us as well. And we, in our turn, pray for the souls in purgatory, as do the saints in heaven. We are all children of God, and like the children in a loving family, we must help one another.

We know that in praying for our loved ones who have died we are helping them. We cannot comprehend death very well, Lord. It remains a mystery, and yet we know that You conquered death in the Resurrection. You taught us that death is passing from this world into eternal life. The Church teaches us that our prayers should go with those who have preceded us in death. Love does not die at the grave. We continue to love those who have died, just as we loved them in life. The way we now have of showing our love is by praying for them. Prayer goes beyond the grave. Prayer shows our love after death. And so we pray for the deceased. Amen.

Wednesday, Fourth Week of Lent

Reflection

"The Lord is my shepherd, and I shall not want," states the psalmist (Psalm 23:1). We are not orphans. We are not alone. God is with us, now and always. And He blesses us as we strive to do His will and make our way in life.

Where Jesus is there is no darkness, even in the blackest night. Where Jesus is there is love. His light and His goodness lead us. Amid our confusion, He shows the way.

Joyce Kilmer, a Catholic convert poet killed in World War I, wrote:

"Because the road was steep and long
And through a dark and lonely land,
God set upon my lips a song
And put a lantern in my hand."

Because Christ guides us and gives us strength, we can work for good in the world. The author John Gardner wrote, "The world is upheld by the veracity of good men; they make the earth wholesome. Life is pleasant and tolerable only because of them." It is because we have so many people who are good and try to make a better world that we are able to make progress on earth.

In every land there is a constant need for good people, good citizens. G.K. Chesterton said, "Genuine democracy is based on the citizen; a mob is many men where there is no citizen." The citizen is a responsible individual who will obey the law whether he is being watched or not. Without such people, there is mob rule and anarchy. Every country and every community needs people who care. There is more to life than to pamper oneself.

The ancient Athenians had a great city because they thought that a person was worthless unless he contributed time and talent to help better the community. The Christian notion is the same. Unfortunately, today we have too many Christians who do not know what a Christian is, or do not care. These are the many passive, listless, nonparticipating people.

Dr. Martin Luther King Jr. said, "Prayer alone is not enough." Prayer is vital, prayer is essential, but there is more to being a Christian than just a person who prays. To pray and do nothing is to be half a Christian. Jesus wants us to pray — and then act. When the man asked Jesus what an individual must do to gain eternal life, our Lord replied, "Love God and love your neighbor" (see Matthew 22:37-39; Mark 12:30-31; Luke 10:27). When we pray, we love God; when we perform good deeds, we love our neighbor. When your neighbor is hungry, it is not enough to say you will pray for him. That is a kind of "cop-out." Jesus tells us to pray for the hungry man — and feed him, as well.

The Benedictine motto is "Orare et Labore," "Pray and Work." We must do both.

Prayer

O Sacred Heart of Jesus, You are the fountain of kindness and mercy, the glowing furnace of love; You are my refuge and sanctuary. My loving Savior, let a little of Your burning fire of love inflame my poor soul. Graciously pour down upon me Your holy blessings and unite my heart to Yours so I may do as You wish.

O heart of Jesus which loves us with a great love, help me to be grateful for Your goodness. Pardon me my sins, O Jesus, heart of mercy, and keep me ever close to You.

Thank You for the great gift of the Eucharist. In Holy Communion we receive You. Divine life comes into our souls, a life that we are not entitled to but which You give to us because of Your graciousness. You are so kind and merciful to come to me and to bless me. Give me a greater love when I receive You in the Eucharist, dear Lord, so that I may be more closely united to You in all things. Amen.

Thursday, Fourth Week of Lent

Reflection

"Let not your hearts be troubled," Jesus said (John 14:1, 27). "Don't be afraid." He told us not to fear failure. If we fail, at least we have tried to do something — and that is what pleases Christ most of all. He blesses us specially every time we try. We put forth the effort, and the rest is in the hands of God. Success or failure is up to Him. We are like the farmer who plants the seed and then awaits the rain. What upsets God are those who do not try, who are the "do-nothing Christians."

When people failed Jesus, He never turned against them. He did not reject Peter who denied Him, but instead made him the head of the Church. He didn't even reject Judas who betrayed Him. Indeed if Judas had asked for forgiveness, Christ would have given it at once, as readily as He forgave Peter and the other Apostles who deserted Him in the Garden of Gethsemane. The Apostles had all bragged that they would defend Jesus and protect Him and give their lives for Him, but when the soldiers came out to arrest Him, they all fled into the night (see Matthew 26:56; Mark 14:50). And yet He quickly forgave them their cowardice. This is very encouraging to us, since like the Apostles we are weak and sometimes faithless.

Though the Apostles did not help Jesus when He needed them the most, He was always there to help them, and He is always with us to help us also. When we ask His aid, He is there.

We should pray that, as with the Apostles, He will change our weakness into strength, that He will change our cowardice into courage. We need Him badly to aid us in our struggle to master our lethargy.

Others need Him as well. We should pray for them. We cannot touch hearts — only Jesus can do that. We should pray then that Jesus will give them the graces they need, and that they will respond. Many souls, we know, are won by the generous prayers of others.

Sometimes older people especially say, "I can't do anything anymore." But, of course, they can. They can pray, which is the most important thing anyone can do. Much prayer is necessary for the success of those in the active apostolate. Good works without prayer simply cannot prosper; the ultimate self-deception in religion is to say, "My work is my prayer." That is nonsense. Jesus, we recall, spent thirty years in prayer before He began His active life. In truth, without prayer what one does is "my work." That is little. What the Christian is interested in doing is Christ's work, and that can only be done if accompanied by a good deal of prayer.

Prayer

We praise You, O God, and we beg Your blessings on those who live in darkness and do not know You. Bless the unfaithful souls who are disloyal to You. Help them to see that by sin they are only hurting themselves. Help too, O God, the poor and hungry, the needy and weak, and those abandoned by all.

Please heal us as You healed those who came to You in Palestine. Heal us in body and soul; heal us in mind and heart. Renew our love for You and others.

O God, You have made me and given me life. You daily, hourly sustain me. For all these great and wonderful gifts I am deeply grateful; I would not be here without You, I could not continue to live without You. Thank You, O God, from the depths of my heart and soul.

You sent Your only Son to save us from sin. He shed His precious blood and gave His life for us on the cross. I cannot thank You enough, O Jesus. You have given us Holy Communion whereby You come into our souls as spiritual food. Thank You.

O Lord, make me contrite in heart. Increase my sorrow for my sins. Amen.

Friday, Fourth Week of Lent

Reflection

St. Augustine said, "Man finds his full development in prayer." God wants us to grow up, spiritually speaking. We are by nature selfish; growing up means becoming more unselfish. Psychiatrists tell us that the first adult act is an unselfish act. When we do something and don't say, "What's in it for me?" we are beginning to mature. The trouble is some people never grow up. Even at 60 or 70 they are selfish and childish, emotionally immature. Is this because they do not pray very much? St. Augustine seems to think so.

Jesus said, "These things I have spoken to you, so that my joy may be in you, and your joy may be full" (John 15:11). Jesus wants us to be happy in life, but selfish people are never happy. They are like spoiled kids all their days.

A grown person looks foolish playing with a little tricycle when he is over 50. We are supposed to grow up and put away the toys of childhood. But, even more, we are supposed to mature emotionally and be more unselfish. We are supposed to be more loving, giving individuals.

To be happy a person must practice self-discipline. We see this in the athlete. He knows well that to gain the victory means a lot of hard work, endless practice and training, sacrifice day after day after day. The fun comes in the game only if there has been great seif-discipline for many days before. The Christian is a spiritual athlete. He denies himself also, for a much greater goal than the player in a game of sports. Penance purifies the soul and makes one a better, more unselfish person. It helps one grow up — and then he knows joy.

In practicing penance we imitate Jesus, who was the most unselfish person who ever lived. We follow Christ up the hill to Calvary on Good Friday, but we also follow Him to the joy of Easter Sunday. Glory comes after sacrifice.

People who do not deny themselves do not grow up, and they are unable to cope with life. Self-control enables us to face life, and self-discipline leads to the exhilarating experiences of victory with Christ.

In doing penance we are not supposed to go around with sad, sour faces in a morose mood. Jesus said, "When you fast do not show it by gloomy looks, as the hypocrites do. They make their faces sad, so they can show off their fasting" (Matthew 6:16).

The Christian, the mature person, one who has grown up and put away his childishness, is to put on a bright and cheerful face and greet people with a pleasant smile. Indeed, being pleasant when one doesn't feel like it is often penance enough. Not boring others with a lot of talk about how badly we feel is a sacrifice that they will appreciate more than you know — and Jesus will appreciate it too. A Christian always complaining is a bad advertisement for Christ, who came to earth to bring the "good news."

Prayer

O Lord Jesus, with tears I look at You hanging on the cross and I am ashamed of all my complaining about my little pains. I know that sin has caused Your terrible suffering. I am sorry for my sins. Your love is so immense, and my love is so pale in comparison. Please increase my love. Please make me a kinder, more unselfish, more mature person. Help me to grow up; don't let me act like a headstrong little kid all my life. And yet I know full well that if I am to improve and be a better person, You must help me. I am weak. I need Your assistance. Be with me always, dear Jesus, guide and direct me. Be with me in my troubles and lead me on through my trials and difficulties. Bless also, Lord, my loved ones. They too need Your help, whether they know it or not.

Especially I beg You, dearest Friend, Lord and Savior, to be with me at the end when I breathe my last sigh. May I die in Your loving arms. Amen.

Saturday, Fourth Week of Lent

Reflection

The world is full of hungry people, hungry in body and hungry in soul. We should do what we can to help them. Jesus rewards those who feed the hungry, because, in doing so, they do it for Him. "I was hungry, and you gave me to eat," Jesus says (Matthew 25:35).

Most of us do not live near people who are hungry in body, but we can give money through our parish to these unfortunate people. Almost all of us, however, live near people who are starving spiritually. They hunger for something — they know not what. They feel empty and are restless and anxious. This is their soul seeking Jesus, but they are not aware of it.

So many people in our society try not to think about their emptiness. They distract themselves with entertainment, seeking an escape in pleasure, drinking, drugs, or anything else they can think of. But in the end they still feel empty, maybe even more so.

We surely should pray for these people, pray that they may be enlightened to understand their problem, that they may come to see that the soul seeks God just as the body hungers for food. For in many ways these people are just as wretched as those who do not have enough to eat. The spiritually starving are well fed in body and hungry in soul.

Let us ask our Lord to help them. And maybe we can even send them a leaflet of prayers in the mail. It is not necessary to put our return address on it, unless we wish to; the main thing is to get into their hands something that will answer their needs. Surely if we saw a person in need of food, we would help him at once. Why are we reluctant to help those in spiritual need? Sometimes we say we don't want to interfere, but that is like saying, "I won't help that drowning man because I don't want to interfere." Jesus is more interested in souls than in bodies. If helping in religion embarrasses us, then sending the prayer leaflet anonymously in the mail answers that problem. The vital thing is to get something to these unfortunate people that will help them. When a person is trapped in a burning building, we concentrate on rescuing him, not on whether he will be embarrassed to be brought out in his underwear. Saving souls is just as important as saving bodies. It is too bad today, but we have become such materialists that even in religion we think the body more important than the soul.

When you help a neighbor in spiritual need you are like the saints. The saints were called "love in action." They worried about souls; they did something to help unhappy people learn of the love of Jesus. By sending people without religion a little prayer pamphlet, we can at least offer them an opportunity to pray, and if they pray, Christ will come to them and help them in ways we cannot even think of. If we but introduce them to Jesus, He will do the rest. But now many people do not know Christ (even though they think they do). Jesus wants us to help Him. Jesus wants us to introduce Him to them.

Prayer

Jesus, I take my religion for granted, and I forget that most people in our society do not know You. If I am a true disciple I must help You by helping them get acquainted with You. Help me to send these people a little prayer pamphlet in the mail. It is not necessary for them to know where it came from; the important thing is that they have it, that they are given an opportunity, an invitation to pray. And if they pray they are halfway home. Help me to see this. Help me to know that to be a Christian means I cannot just sit on my hands and do nothing; I am supposed to help You, Lord. Maybe I can get my Christian friends to do the same. In doing something positive like this — instead of worrying about the lack of religion in the world — I am pleasing You, dearest Jesus. You have done so much for me; help me to do this little thing for You. We send "Care" packages to people physically hungry; help me to send a package of love, a little leaflet of prayers, to a neighbor who is spiritually hungry. Hunger of soul is just as bad as hunger of body. Help me to see this. Amen.

Fifth Week

Fifth Sunday of Lent

Reflection

"I thirst," Jesus said on the cross (John 19:28). He was physically thirsty, but He was willing to endure this, for He refused the wine offered Him. His real thirst was spiritual; He thirsted for souls.

In the world today Jesus continues to thirst for souls. However, since He now no longer walks in the world as He once did, He needs our help. When He lived in Palestine He spent His days reaching out and touching and healing people in body and soul. But since His return to heaven, this is our mission, to carry on His work. This indeed was His last command to us, to go out and tell others about Him, so that He could then come to them and bless them with His graces.

We are His apostles today. We are to tell people about Him and His love. But do we? Haven't many Christians turned into selfish individuals, praying only for themselves and their loved ones and ignoring all those others who do not know of the love of Jesus? This unfortunately is the present Christian posture in America, especially among many Catholics. Someone called this "telephone-booth Christianity." Christians go into the spiritual tele-

phone booth and shut the door and talk to God about themselves. But is this truly being a Christian? Is that what
Christ told us to do? And can we ignore Christ and His
command and still pretend to be a good Christian?

The Christian must follow Christ. Did Christ think only
of himself? Of course not; He spent all His days thinking
of others and helping them. How is it then that we modern
Christians have become so selfish and self-centered? We
must have taken a wrong turn somewhere. We have to get
back on the right road; we have to once more walk with
Christ and love Him by doing what He has told us to do.

It is the saints who can show us the way, for the saints
never took the wrong road. The saints never just talked
about love — they did something as well. They, like Jesus,
gave love away by helping the needy. Do you? The saints
shared with others the most precious gift they had —
Jesus. They told others about Jesus. The Christian cannot
be a spiritual miser and keep the tremendous gift of Christ
all to himself. We must do what Jesus told us to do, if we
are to please Him. And He told us to share His divine message with others. "Go out," He said, "and tell everyone
about me" (see Mark 16:15). Do you do this? Are you a
real Christ-follower if you don't?

Most people immediately say they don't know how to
talk religion and they don't want to interfere with their
neighbors. All right, then go to the parish or the church
goods store and get a little leaflet of prayers and, as was
suggested yesterday, put their address on it (and no return
address) and send it through the mail. You are offering
them a way to know Jesus. Isn't prayer the way we all
come to know Christ?

Prayer

Lord, do not let me be a selfish Christian, for a self-centered Christian is no Christian at all. Do not let me in prayer just think of myself and my needs and those of my loved ones. Help me to pray for others. I can start by praying for the poor souls in purgatory. In prayer I can reach out to them and help them. And I can pray for the people in my neighborhood who do not go to church, or go so rarely it is the same thing. They do not know You, Jesus. Enlighten them. Show them that You are the answer to all their worries. I pray for the hungry people of the world, those who are hungry in body and also those who suffer from hunger of soul, because they are ignorant of You, Jesus, their closest, dearest Friend. And I pray for the people who are not free, who live under dictators and who suffer from oppression and persecution. Bless them all, dear Lord. You have been so good to me, have blessed me so often in so many ways; please also bless these others who need You. Amen.

Monday, Fifth Week of Lent

Reflection

"You who seek God, let your hearts be merry," the Bible tells us (Psalm 69:33). We long for God. The Old Testament prophet said, "He who walks in darkness, to whom no light appears, let him trust in the name of the Lord, let him rely upon God" (Isaiah 50:10).

We turn to God for we know He is our Father and loves us dearly, as a good father loves his children and cherishes them and holds them close to his heart. We turn to God in our needs. Abraham Lincoln during some of the darkest days of the Civil War said, "I often go down on my knees because I know nowhere else to turn." We go to God, because there is nowhere else. If our heavenly Father will not help us, who will do so? But, of course, we know He will help us. A good father always takes care of his children, and God is the best Father.

We trust in our dear Father and thank Him for His graciousness in sending His Son to save us. Before Christ came there was little joy on earth. A pall of pessimism was over the land; melancholy filled the hearts of all. But our Lord brought hope and happiness. With Christ there was gladness, for He proclaimed the "good news" to the people. Pascal wrote, "No one is happy except the true Christian."

In our world we find a good deal of gloom, for today many ignore God and think only of worldly success, which never really satisfies the human heart. Many live like pagans today. They may say they believe in God, but they do not act like it. And, as Jesus told us, we are to be judged by deeds and not by mere words. Modern pagans are putting all kinds of false gods ahead of the true God: pleasure, money, power, popularity. But in doing so, after the first excitement is over, they are emptyhearted. In disregarding God they take the sunshine out of life; they lose the joy of walking with Jesus; they "shout down the melodies of heaven."

We live in a noisy, rush-rush society; the bustle of modern life crowds Christ out of the picture. William Wordsworth wrote, "The world is too much with us; late and soon, / Getting and spending, we lay waste our powers. . . .'' This is what happens when material concerns dominate us. People fall so much in love with their possessions that soon they no longer own them but are owned by their possessions.

The heart of humanity longs for Jesus and His joy. It can never be satisfied with the trinkets and gadgets of life. We were made for greater things. All these are but distractions and petty playthings. Our soul desires more, much more than the mere toys of life — our soul desires our dearest Friend, Jesus.

Prayer

Spirit of wisdom and understanding, enlighten us to know Jesus better. Holy Spirit, give us courage to follow Jesus' way of love. Let mercy direct our daily actions; give us the knowledge we need to solve our problems.

Spirit of God, renew our faith, hope and charity each day. Fill our lives with Your goodness, and help us to pass on Your goodness and love to others, beginning with our own family. Help us to appreciate the wonders and beauty of nature all about us. We so often take for granted Your many magnificent gifts. We are like spoiled children who never thank You for what we have. We grab up Your munificent gifts and demand more. We are so unseeing and so often ungrateful, so lacking in wisdom, kindness and gratitude. Help us, please.

Eternal God, holy and good, glorious and blessed, strengthen my faith, for I am weak; guide my steps, for I am spiritually blind; give me the gift of gratitude, for I so rarely am appreciative. Lord, I cry out to You with all my heart: I need You. Amen.

Tuesday, Fifth Week of Lent

Reflection

"A man must have faith — or he has nothing." This was said by a former British prime minister. There are too many difficulties in life to try to go it alone. And the wonderful thing is — we don't have to. Jesus is with us every day and every hour of every day. He is with us here and now, to help us on our journey.

As we go along in life, we need Jesus more and more. Without Him, the tensions and pressures pull us apart.

People who put their trust in money are not happy. You can't buy happiness; it's not for sale. Neither can you buy love or friends.

Happiness comes from God. The saints were the happiest people of all because they lived close to Christ. Many of them had problems, but they walked through the storms of life with peace in their hearts, for they were serving God. Jesus was with them, and they were happy.

With Jesus there is love, and the friend of Christ is a loving person. He has many friends; maybe not much money but many friends. Friends are vital for happy living; to have friends, you have to be a friend.

Some people sit around filled with self-pity, complaining that they are lonely. The trouble is they are self-centered. They don't lift a finger to be friendly; they want people to come to them. But if you want friends you must reach out and be friendly to others.

A proud person doesn't have friends. He is too selfish. Rich people do not have friends; they buy friends, but this is the furthest thing from real friendship. Friendship is based on mutual consideration and a reciprocal respect.

We are certain that the Blessed Mother at Nazareth had many friends. Why? Because she was so gentle and kind. We know that no needy person who came to her door was ever turned away. She welcomed the needy with a smile; she brought them in, no matter how many, and fed them even if it meant less for the Holy Family. At the table in their little home there was always room for one more. She smiled and gave special care to the small children and made them feel at home, perhaps letting them play with the little wooden toys that Joseph had made for Jesus when He was a child. She made all who came through her door feel wanted and special; she treated them as if it was an honor to have them and a privilege to serve them.

Prayer

Bless the people of America, dear Lord. Bless our farmers, who provide us with food. Bless the merchants who sell and the workers who make the many fine things that we have. Bless the doctors and nurses who help the sick, the priests who bring us the graces of God, the teachers who train our youngsters, the lawyers who see that justice is done. Bless the postmen and the firemen and the policemen and all others who serve us. Bless all, dear Lord, who make our life pleasant and enjoyable. What a cold and bleak place our community would be without the help of these and so many other good people. Bless especially the people who volunteer and give their time freely to others. They bring a special blessing on our town with their kindness.

Help me to be more like the Blessed Mother and to reach out to the needy. You were so gracious, O Mary. You assisted others quietly and efficiently and always with a smile. You were not only a mother to the Child Jesus; you were like a mother to the whole community. If there was anyone sick or in need, you were there. Be a mother to me also, dear Mary. Amen.

Wednesday, Fifth Week of Lent

Reflection

One of the dearest names in the world to Christians is Mary. On the cross, even though He was in agony, Jesus gave us His Mother to be our Mother also. How thoughtful He was. How amazing that even while He was suffering so, He thought of us. What a wonderful gift He gave us in Mary. She teaches us how to pray, for we remember her saying, "Be it done unto me according to thy word" (Luke 1:38). Whatever God wanted, she wanted. This is the perfect prayer. A child imitates his mother; we should in prayer imitate our Blessed Mother.

A mother is a teacher, and Mary teaches us generosity. Even when it was told to her that she had been chosen from among all creatures to be the mother of the Messiah, the highest honor possible, her thoughts went to her cousin Elizabeth. The angel had said that Elizabeth was to have a child in her old age, and Mary knew that she would need help. Thoughtless of self, Mary set out on the long journey to the hill country of Judea to be with Elizabeth to assist her (see Luke 39ff).

We know too that Mary prays for us constantly; a mother is always praying for her children. Her love never fails us. A mother never gives up on her child, even though everyone else may do so. Mary is our guide and our comfort and our consolation. She is our best intercessor with her divine Son. Just as Jesus came to us through Mary, we can go to Jesus through Mary.

With Mary praying for us and helping us, we need not be afraid. A child is not fearful when his mother is near. We, like a child, are often unthinking and weak. But that is especially when a mother is around, to help the smallest child, to help the sick child.

Sometimes we want to give up and turn back. Especially when we grow weary because the way is long and uphill. And in our difficulties we find it hard to pray. Then it is time for us, like a little child, to run to the arms of our Mother. We know that Mary will pick us up and take us in her warm and loving arms and comfort us and carry us on our way. In times of trouble we should always turn to her.

Our heart cries out to Mary when we struggle and we cannot see. When we are trembling and tearful, we call to her to help us and to hold us, as we did with our own mother when we were little. We beg for her mercy; we ask her to have pity on us. All we can give her is our weakness, but if we commit this into her holy hands she will be there and she will help us; she will wrap her motherly arms around us and hold us to her loving heart, just as she did with Jesus when He was a little baby.

Prayer

Dear Blessed Mother, I love you. Some people sometimes say we love you too much, but that is foolish — none of us can begin to love you as much as Jesus did. So we don't have to worry about that. Our worry is that we may not love you enough.

Jesus has blessed us twice. Not only did He give us a good mother in this life, but He has given us a mother in heaven, the Blessed Mother. When Mary asked Jesus to help someone on earth He never refused her. Who can refuse his mother when there is something he can do? And now that the Blessed Mother is even closer to Christ in heaven, she can help us even more. It is your delight, dear Mary, to help your children. A mother always thinks more of helping her children than of herself, and our dear Mother in heaven is no exception. I am sure of that, O loving Mary. And so I entrust myself and my loved ones to your gracious care. With you looking after us everything will be all right. Amen.

Thursday, Fifth Week of Lent

Reflection

Jesus told His disciples that the time had come. As He had foretold more than once, He must now go up to Jerusalem where He would be arrested, tortured and put to death. This greatly saddened the Apostles. They understood so little of what He tried to tell them. And Peter told Jesus that He must not speak like that. But Jesus turned to him and said to Peter that his thoughts were those of Satan and not of God. He must go up to Jerusalem so that His great mission might be fulfilled.

How courageous Jesus was in starting out for Jerusalem for the last time, knowing that torture, humiliation and death awaited Him. Yet He set His face toward the city, going out in front of the Apostles, and He would not turn back. This was His destiny; this was His vocation; for this He had come into the world; to save the people from sin, to proclaim by word and deed His kingdom of love. The Apostles halfheartedly followed at a distance. As Monsignor Ronald Knox said of them, "They could not understand Him, but they could not leave Him."

Jesus in heading toward Jerusalem and death — death for us upon the cross — was showing us again, and this time in a most dramatic way, His love for us. "Who else," He can say to each of us, "has ever died for you? Who else has ever loved you so much that he willingly endured the horrible suffering of the crucifixion for you?"

Jesus says to us, "Please let me give my great love to you — it will bring you blessings beyond belief." How can we refuse Him? How can we ignore Him and turn our back on Him to play with the toys of this life? Are we such little children, so small in mind and heart, that we cannot realize that in disregarding Jesus' offer of love we are throwing away the greatest thing that can happen to us in this life? We are casting it away for a few gadgets or for a few seconds of fleeting pleasure.

People must be out of their minds to reject the love of Christ, which can only bring us love and joy in life.

We must pray for light to see how great Christ's love is, and the courage to open our hearts to Him. We simply do not know Jesus, if we can walk away from Him for trinkets. Not only must the true Christian pray so that he will truly know our Lord, but also that he may be Christ's instrument in the world to spread His love and goodness.

It is our duty to give others hope in their humdrum and

troubled lives, the hope of Jesus. It is our calling as Christians to show — and not just talk about — the kindness of Christ. We pray that we may be worthy instruments of our Savior in the world. We are not gifted people, but often the gifted in their pride do not help God. Monsignor Ronald Knox wrote that those through the years closest to Christ "have not been learned people who know how to argue religion, but simple people who know how to live it." And so in humility, small as we are, we offer ourselves to the Lord so that He can achieve things through us.

Prayer

Dear Lord, help me to be, in the words of the "Prayer of St. Francis," an instrument of Your peace. Use me to show others Your love. Direct me to those in need. Enlighten me so that I can help them and give them hope. There are so many poor people in this world, not poor in material possession but poor in the things of the spirit. They are anxious and restless. Help me to help them. Show me, dearest Jesus, the way to tell them of Your love and goodness, to show them that You are the answer to life. As the poet W.H. Auden said, "We are in God's hands, or we are nowhere." You, dear Lord, have blessed me with Your truth and Your love. But You have not given me these priceless gifts for myself alone. You wish me to pass them on. O Lord, help me to do this. Help me to be an apostle for You in our troubled, sick and weary world. Amen.

Friday, Fifth Week of Lent

Reflection

As Jesus heads toward Jerusalem to take up His cross and give His life for us, we reflect upon the cross. It is a mystery, and yet He teaches us that our victory is in the cross. By His suffering on the cross Jesus saved the world; by our suffering we can learn more compassion for others and become better people. We really do not know about life unless we have experienced pain. No one has ever accomplished anything in life without suffering. God took the risk of giving us free will, which means that in pain we can either curse Him or offer it up as a prayer. Man is at his best accepting trials in life. It is not easy, to be sure, but it is the sign of greatness of soul. Many people indeed are saved through suffering. Jesus said, "Unless the grain of wheat falls into the ground and dies, it remains alone" (John 12:24). We are like the seed which dies in order to become a fruitful and wonderful plant. This is what suffering does for us: we die to childishness and selfishness and are reborn as mature, unselfish adults. Suffering makes us grow up, unless we reject it. And when we suffer we are very close to Christ. In truth, in suffering we join in redeeming mankind.

The suffering Christian, one who accepts his pain with resignation, is the greatest representative of Christ we have in this world. Many people today do not know Jesus, but in us — in knowing us and seeing that we do not let the sorrows of this world overwhelm us — they see Jesus.

It is not only in suffering that we follow Jesus and show ourselves as His ambassadors, but actually in all things that we do. Non-Christians are watching us constantly, even those who say religion is worthless.

We need to pray that we may more faithfully imitate our Lord. St. Vincent de Paul said, "I pray God that He may give me the grace to retain the spirit of gentleness. Bitterness only embitters." Those without religion are judging us not by what we say but by what we do. They do not hear us, but they watch us. Ralph Waldo Emerson said, "I cannot hear what you say because what you do thunders so loudly in my ears." It is our kindness that shows we are true to Christ. Jesus said, "For I have given you an example, that as I have done to you, so you do also" (John 13:15). What did Jesus do? He spent all His days being kind to people. He never turned away anyone who came to Him. This is our model. We are to imitate Christ. He did so many wonderful things to help people that St. Peter gave up telling them all and finally summarized His life by saying, "[He] went about doing good" (Acts 10:38). Can we do less and be worthy of the name of Christian?

Prayer

Dear Jesus, bless my home and family. Shower us with Your gracious graces, for we are in need of Your help. Help all who are in need; help those especially who are sad and suffering because the bottom has dropped out of their lives. Be there beside them when they try to pick up the pieces.

I place my loved ones in particular in the special care of our dear Blessed Mother. I know that she will take care of them. I know that like a loving mother she will help them especially in the confusion of life. I entrust them to you, dear Mary; bless them with your wonderful love, protect them and assist them this day and every day. And please help me too. I place myself under your protection in a most special way. Assist me, as we pray in the Hail Mary, now and at the hour of my death. I am weak and in need now; and at the hour of my death I will need you, Mother, most of all. I love you, Blessed Mother, and I know that you love me. I am weak, but a mother loves her smallest and weakest child most of all. Be with me. Amen.

Saturday, Fifth Week of Lent

Reflection

Jesus, You are now nearing Jerusalem to give Your life on the cross to save us. You suffered so much for us, dear Jesus. You ask us to suffer a little for You. We pray that we may do so; we pray that we may endure our trials in life. Many times we cannot pray very well; we are pretty pedestrian when it comes to prayer, but at least we can offer up our sufferings as a prayer, and we know that is pleasing to God. We do not really comprehend pain; it is one of the mysteries of life. What we do know is that when we join our sufferings to those of Christ on the cross it is not wasted but is a prayer and does good for us and for others.

When we resign ourselves to our pain — pain we can do nothing about — it is a prayer not unlike the prayer of Jesus on the cross. By accepting our difficulties we are making up for our past sins and helping others in need, both the living and the dead. Every person in the world has a cross to carry. Some have a cross that we can see; others have a cross on the inside that is known only to them and to God. But everyone has a cross. And it is how we carry our cross that counts. Small-hearted people rebel and carry their cross cursing God, but people who are big in heart bear their difficulties with resignation. Small souls turn bitter in time of trouble; the large in heart grow greater still.

The cross comes to everyone differently — to some as sickness; to others, family troubles; to still others, financial difficulties, and on and on. We pray that Jesus will help us to carry our cross as Simon helped Him on the way to Calvary. Sometimes a person works hard for others and is repaid with ingratitude and ridicule. Such people need Jesus and His love to assist them, and we pray for them and for all who are having a hard time in life. We pray for those who have friends who are disloyal to them. How hard this is to bear! But then Jesus knows all about such heartaches, and He will especially help us over these rough times.

When we accept our sickness or loneliness or the loss of a dear one, Jesus is closer to us than at any other time. And in not rebelling we imitate Christ, who said, "Father, if it be possible let this cup pass away from me; yet not as I will, but as you will it" (Matthew 26:39; see Mark 14:36, Luke 22:42). Jesus did not wish to undergo the tragic suffering and agony of the cross; His human nature totally opposed it, and yet He endured all this heartache and hardship for love of us. So we should strive to accept our suffering, far smaller, for love of Him and to help others. In doing so we bring new blessings to the world, so badly in need of God's help. No suffering offered up is in vain. If accepted in the name of Christ it is a glorious prayer. And we should remember the words of St. Paul, "I have suffered the loss of all things, and count them as waste, in order to gain Christ'' (Philippians 3:8).

Prayer

O Jesus, I need You. I need the spiritual strength and courage that only You can give. I cannot begin to solve all my problems alone. I am so in need of Your help. My troubles worry me and upset me; help me to trust You more. I need more faith and more hope in You. I am so weak. Help me to calm down; help me to be more loving. I need to grow in kindness. At times I am a very poor Christian. Come to me and bring Your blessings, so that I will have peace of soul and Your love in my heart. How can I help others without Your love?

Make me a more giving person, and help me to listen more and not to talk so much. I need to be less critical and sour; I need to be more smiling and pleasant. But You are going to have to give me the graces to change. You are always with me, I know, and You have helped me so many times before. I know You will help me now. Assist me then, Lord, to do the kind thing for others and to say the kind word. Don't let me say mean and spiteful things to my family and others; let me rather show them Your love. Amen.

Holy Week

Palm Sunday

Reflection

Jesus approached Jerusalem for the last time (see Matthew 21:1-10, Mark 11:1-10, Luke 19:29-38, John 12:12-18). When the people saw Him they were so happy that they rushed out to greet Him. Spontaneously they broke off palm branches from the trees and waved them, and joyfully cried out, "Hosanna, hosanna! Hosanna to the Son of David. Blessed is he who comes in the name of the Lord. Hosanna in the highest!"

The festive crowd triumphantly escorted Him into the city. Some visitors, watching the procession, said, "Who is this?" They were told, "It is Jesus, the prophet from Nazareth of Galilee."

The Apostles paraded proudly alongside Jesus, basking in His glory. But a few nights later, when the temple guards came to arrest Him, the Apostles all ran away. We are like that, like the Apostles, often fair-weather friends. When Jesus is giving us things we are wonderful companions, but when He needs our help we are nowhere around. We rejoice in our religion when it makes us feel good, but when it hurts, when it costs us something, we run away.

Following the Palm Sunday procession, Jesus went to

the great temple. There He saw the merchants buying and selling things, making money out of religion, and this angered Him. He cried out, "It is written, 'My house is a house of prayer,' and you have made it a den of thieves" (Matthew 21:13, Mark 11:17, Luke 19:46; see Jeremiah 7:11). He pushed over their tables and upset their chairs and chased them away.

The temple must be a place of prayer. Business owned all the city, but, never satisfied, these money-crazed merchants had now invaded even the sacred precincts of the house of God. Jesus would not have it.

The Pharisees watched Jesus force the businessmen out of the temple, and in their hearts they approved, wishing they had had enough courage to do so. But what was most on their minds was getting rid of Christ. They were crazy with jealousy because of His popularity, and especially after the great show of love of the people in the procession of palms. They had never even thought of doing a thing like that for the Pharisees. So instead of praising Jesus they used this as an opportunity to turn against Him again. "By what authority do you do this? Who gave you this right?" the Pharisees asked angrily (see Matthew 21:23, Mark 11:27, Luke 20:1).

But as usual Jesus took their question, by which they sought to trap Him, and turned it against them. They tried to make Him look foolish, and they ended up looking foolish themselves. This infuriated them all the more, and made them even more determined to get rid of Him.

Before Jesus, the Pharisees had been the religious leaders and teachers. The people honored them and bowed to them and brought them gifts and kissed their hands. They were proud men, and they loved it. But now this man from Galilee had come and the people had deserted the

Pharisees and gone to listen to Him. They could not stand this. They must destroy Him.

Prayer

Jesus, dear Friend, You are willing to give Your life for me. How can I ever begin to repay You? A lesser person, when he learned that the leaders were plotting to destroy him, would have run away. But You stood firm. With Your magnificent courage You stayed on in Jerusalem, though Your days were numbered — and no one knew that better than You.

I am so grateful that You were willing to endure so much for love of me. I know from the events of Holy Week how very, very much You love me. I ask You to bless me and my family. Help me to be kinder to those I love in my own home. So often I am pleasant at work or out in public or at a party, but I am unpleasant at home, among the people I love the most. Let me be more loving toward my family. Permit me to give my best to the people I love the most. If I must be angry, let it be outside my home. How foolish to be courteous everywhere else and to everybody else except to my family. Never let me take my loved ones for granted. "Charity begins at home." May our family always be loving and loyal to one another. Amen.

Monday of Holy Week

Reflection

Jesus knew the Pharisees, blind with envy, were determined to get Him out of the way, by fair means or foul.

They, of course, like many people, fixed up their con-
science for this. As the proverb says, "The wish is father
to the thought." They wished Him out of the way so that
the people would return to them and honor them once
more. Proud men live on popularity and applause. Now
they said that to get rid of Jesus was their patriotic duty.
He must be put to death because He was teaching the people a new way. How often in history individuals wrap
themselves in the flag in order to get what they want for
themselves!

Jesus knew all this, but He still stayed on in Jerusalem. He was exceedingly brave. He knew that His vocation
as Redeemer was to suffer for the people. He would not
flinch or flee. And in the meantime He continued to teach
openly. He so loved the people that He wanted them to
know the "good news" that He had brought from heaven to
earth, and so He used every hour of His last days to tell
them again and again how much God loved them, how
much God loves all people.

He was more than aware that jealousy had crazed the
minds of the Pharisees and their associates; jealousy can
do this, as Shakespeare shows us in *Othello*. The
Pharisees hated Jesus for taking the people away from
them, but, of course, it was really the teaching of the
Pharisees that drove people away. They proclaimed an
absurd, puritanical, harsh and severe religion; Jesus
spoke only of love. The Pharisees, though, were blind to all
this. They were the rightful religion teachers, and the people must listen to them. They were determined to do anything to get the people back — even murder. They must do
this, they said, "for the welfare of the people" (see John
11:50-52). Any nonsense made sense to them in their highly
agitated state.

Jesus, teaching in the temple precincts daily, continued to tell of love. On one occasion as He sat there He looked up and saw a poor widow put two pennies into the poor box. Just before that a number of pompous rich men had put in a good deal of money with great showmanship. Jesus said, "Let me tell you, this poor woman has put in more than all the others." Why? Because they gave for show what they would never miss, but she gave from her food money. (See Mark 12:41-44, Luke 21:1-4.)

Continuing to teach, He told the people about the farmer who had two sons and asked them to help him. One said, "Yes," but never went; the other said, "No," but then regretted it and went out in the field and worked. Jesus said that the story showed that God is interested in deeds, not words — in what we do, not what we say. He concluded, addressing those who talk and do nothing, "I say to you, the sinners and harlots will enter the kingdom of God before you." (See Matthew 21:28-32.)

Prayer

Dear Jesus, these are strong words, but I know they are true. Too often we Christians seem to think our religion is a discussion club. We have too many who talk religion but do not practice it. Help me not to be like that. Help me to show my love by deeds and not by words. The little kid who tells his mother night and day how much he loves her and then steals cookies when she doesn't want him to — he doesn't love her, he is only saying words. The boyfriend who tells his girl how much he loves her but never takes her anyplace nor brings her gifts — she soon realizes he is all just talk. Don't let me be "only talk" in religion. People like that are phony; they are hypocrites.

Mother Teresa of Calcutta cannot preach very well, but she is out in the street every day picking up the dying and taking them to her little hospital. She does not have to talk; she shows her love. Please give me the grace to be more like that. Amen.

Tuesday of Holy Week

Reflection

The people each day gathered to hear Jesus; they loved Him and found joy in His message of love. He was like sunshine coming into their drab, dull lives. But sitting amid all this adulation, He knew well His days were numbered, for the Pharisees, standing in the shadows, were plotting against Him. They had nothing but disdain for Him since He had taken the people away from them. The only thing that kept them from seizing Him right away was fear of the people. They loved Him so much, the Pharisees knew, that if they tried to arrest Him a riot would break out.

The Pharisees represent all those in every age who, while pretending piety, use religion for their own gain. They are the false prophets Jesus spoke about, self-seekers rather than servants of God. And now the Pharisees were out to destroy innocence itself.

Our Lord had often predicted all this, but the Apostles would not accept it. It must never happen. He told them He was to go to Jerusalem to suffer many things from the elders, scribes and chief priests and be put to death, but on the third day He would rise again. But the Apostles did not want Him to talk like that; it filled them with fear and sadness. Finally, but a few days ago, as His time drew near, He had said, "Now we are going up to Jerusalem, and the Son of Man will be betrayed to the chief priests and scribes and they will condemn him to death, and they will deliver him over to the Gentiles to be mocked and scourged and crucified; and on the third day he will rise again" (Matthew 20:18-19; see Mark 10:33-34, Luke 18:31-33). At this the Apostles were dismayed and didn't know what to say. At length Thomas said they should go with Him and die with Him (see John 11:16).

Now teaching daily at the temple, Jesus emphasized, as He had done so often before, that those who followed Him must be servants and not masters. He said that among the worldly-minded the leaders lord it over the others, but "not so among you" (Matthew 20:25-26, Mark 10:42-43, Luke 22:25-26). Indeed, the teaching of Jesus "turned the world upside down." With the Christian, the rule that "might makes right" must not apply. Jesus said, "On the contrary whoever wishes to be great among you shall be your servant . . . even as the Son of Man has not come to be served but to serve, to give his life as a ransom for many" (Matthew 20:26-28; see Mark 10:43-45). On the following Thursday, at the Last Supper, He showed them what He meant. He rose from the supper "and laid aside his garments and, taking a towel, girded himself. Then he poured water into a basin and began to wash the feet of the disciples, and to dry them with the towel with which he was girded" (John 13:5).

Afterwards Jesus said, "Do you know what I have done for you? You call me Master and Lord, and you say well, for so I am. If, therefore, I the Lord and Master wash your feet, you also ought to wash the feet of one another. . . . As I have done to you, so you also should do" (John 13:12-15).

Prayer

Jesus, You have told us that as Christians we must serve one another, and that the first shall be last, and the highest must serve the lowest. This is not the way of the world, You told us, but this is the way it must be among Your followers. Help me to learn this important lesson. We Christians are so much in the world that it is very easy to take on the ways of the world. But with You it is different. Never let me forget that, Lord. The Christian is a servant, no matter how high or important he is in the world or in the Church. We must serve others, and especially we must serve those who are in need, as You pointed out so wonderfully in the Parable of the Good Samaritan.

These are so beautiful, Your teachings; they had to have come from heaven. Your message is so sublime that no mere human could have invented it. Your words are so magnificent that they have to be divine. Even if You never worked a miracle, we would know Your divinity from Your teachings. "No man ever spoke like this man" (John 7:46). Thank You, Lord. Amen.

Wednesday of Holy Week

Reflection

This was the day that Judas played right into the hands of the Pharisees. They were looking for a way to do away with Jesus, but they feared the people. They would have to take Him secretly, but they didn't know how. Then Judas went to them — just what they wanted. He asked, "What are you willing to give me if I will deliver him to you?" (Matthew 26:15; see Mark 14:10, Luke 20:20).

How wonderful for the Pharisees. They would be able to seize Jesus, arrest Him, try Him and have Him on the way to the hill of execution before the ordinary people of the city were awake.

They carefully counted out 30 pieces of silver for Judas. The betrayer grabbed it up and left. No doubt after he was gone they laughed and rejoiced and patted one another on the back. They at last were to have the trouble-maker in their hands. Now they would be rid of Him, and then they would be the religious leaders again, honored and praised once more, as was their right.

Why did Judas betray Jesus? We do not know. There is mention that he was the treasurer of the group and had grown too fond of money. But the reason had to be more than that. Perhaps he was one of those who became disillusioned when Jesus would not lead a rebellion against the Romans and free the Jewish people once more. The Jews were a fiercely independent nation and they hated their overlords with a passion. When Jesus came on the scene, He was a leader, and the only kind of leader many wanted was a George Washington to throw out the oppressors. Once, the Gospel tells us (John 6:15), they tried to take Jesus by force and make Him their king and rebel leader. But He left and hid out on the mountainside. So when it became apparent He was not going to fit in with their plans, they gave up on Him as a dreamer. When He said, "My kingdom is not of this world," they left Him. In a way, we can see their point of view. If America was conquered by a foreign power, we would hate every minute of it; we would wake up every morning wondering how we could throw out the enemy and be a free land once more. We Americans love our liberty so much that if we lost it we could think of nothing else except how to regain it. The Jews were the same way, and perhaps Judas was one of these. And so Judas, after giving up on Jesus, decided he might as well make a little money before he "bailed out."

Yet we should not be too harsh on Judas. Before we condemn him too much, let us look at ourselves. He is not the only one who ever betrayed our Lord. That, in fact, is what we also do when we sin. And at least Judas got 30 pieces of silver. What do we get? A few moments of fleeting pleasure perhaps.

Prayer

Jesus Lord, forgive me for betraying You with my sins. Judas sold out on the best Friend he ever had. But in sin we do the same. Loyalty is such a beautiful virtue, but I am ashamed to say, Lord, I am not always loyal to You. Many times I want my own way, against Your way. Too often I go my way and forget and ignore You, dear Jesus. And then it is that, like Judas, I betray You. Forgive me for my sins. Help me to be more faithful to You, as was your dear Blessed Mother. No wonder You love her so much. When all Your friends ran away, she remained faithful. She never deserted You. She followed You to the bitter end and stood with You as You died. The crowd was yelling insults, but she would die with You before she would leave You. Teach me, dear Mary, how to be more faithful to your Son. Amen.

Holy Thursday

Reflection

At the Last Supper Jesus prayed to the Father, "I have made known the truths you gave me to those who have followed me" (see John 17:6-8). Jesus prayed for the Apostles. Then there was a great silence in the upper room. The most solemn moment of all had come. Jesus said, "I greatly desired to eat this meal with you before I suffer" (Luke 22:15). He took bread and blessed it and broke it and said, "This is my body" (Matthew 26:26, Mark 14:22; see Luke 22:19). He took the chalice and said, "This is my blood of the new covenant, which will be shed for many for the forgiveness of sins" (Matthew 26:28, Mark 14:24; see Luke 22:20). He added, "Do this in remembrance of me" (Luke 22:19). He gave the Eucharist to the Apostles as spiritual food for their souls.

In instituting this Holy Sacrament, Jesus gave us one of the greatest gifts God has ever given to man. By means of this ingenious gift, one that only a divine mind could conceive, Jesus would remain with us, even after He returned to the Father. He did not want to leave us orphans; He loved us so much He wished to stay with us. And so He gave us the Eucharist, mystery of mysteries, whereby Christ unites us to himself and gives us nourishment for our souls.

He chose this night, the night before He died, the most solemn moment of His life, to give us His most wonderful gift, himself. He had promised it before more than once, the Bread of Heaven. Now He gives us himself in this

Blessed Sacrament; He comes to us hidden from the sight of mere earthly eyes.

We learn of Christ far better by receiving Holy Communion than from listening to the lectures of great theologians.

As we wander in the wilderness of life, like the Jews wandering in the desert, we look to Christ for help. God gave the Jews manna from heaven in the desert to nourish them. In the New Testament Jesus gives us a new Bread of Heaven to sustain our souls. In the Old Testament journey of the Jews, God assured the people of His presence in the cloud above their tent of worship, the Tabernacle. In the new religion our Lord gives us His loving presence in the tabernacle of the altar.

Christ comes to us in Holy Communion, bringing His love, peace, joy and spiritual strength. How blessed we are; how good Jesus is to us.

Every Mass is a reenactment of the Last Supper which Jesus celebrated with His beloved Apostles. The Eucharist again is consecrated on our altars, in obedience to the command of Christ, "Do this in memory of me" (Luke 22:19). And Jesus in Communion then enters our hearts.

Prayer

St. Thomas Aquinas long ago gave us one of our most beautiful prayers to be recited after Holy Communion:

"I give You thanks, O Holy Lord, Father Almighty, Eternal God, who have granted, not for any merit of mine, but solely out of the goodness of Your mercy to satisfy me a sinner, Your unworthy servant, with the precious Body and Blood of Your Son, our Lord, Jesus Christ. I pray that this Holy Communion be a saving plea for me unto forgiveness. May it be for me an increase of faith and good will. May it be the emptying out of my vices, the extinction of all concupiscence and lust, an increase of charity and patience, of humility and obedience, and of all virtues; a strong defense against the snares of all enemies, visible and invisible; the perfect quieting of all my evil impulses, both in body and spirit. May this Holy Communion be for me a firm cleaving to You, the one true God, and a pledge of a blessed destiny in heaven. I ask You please, O God, that You grant me, a sinner, the grace to participate in Your wondrous heavenly banquet, where You, with Your Son and the Holy Spirit, are for Your saints true light, the fullness of contentment, eternal joy, gladness without end and perfect bliss. I beg this through Christ, our Lord. Amen.''

Good Friday

Reflection

The terrible ordeal of Calvary consists of suffering beyond words. Jesus hangs on the cross in horrible agony. His hands and feet are nailed, His body covered with blood, His head crowned with piercing thorns. Many believe that crucifixion is the most terrible kind of torture ever invented by evil-minded men.

Why did Christ choose this excruciating way to die? One reason surely must be that He was determined once and for all to show us how much He loves us. No one can look upon the crucifix and deny Christ's love. All one can say in meditating before the crucifix is that Jesus loves me more than anyone else in the world does. Who else has given his life for me; who else has suffered such bitter agony for me?

Perhaps before Jesus, in Old Testament times, people could sometimes wonder, because of their troubles, if God loved them; but after Good Friday no one can seriously ask that question.

Jesus could have satisfied for our sins by saying "Yes" to the Father, since man had destroyed our friendship with God by saying "No" to Him. But that was not enough for Jesus. His love for us is too great, and He gave His life and suffered untold pain to show that love.

Amazingly, even on the cross Jesus was thinking of others. His body was broken and He could hardly breathe and yet He said, "Father, forgive them for they know not what they do" (Luke 23:34). He saw His dear Mother standing there, and He gave her to John to care for, and He gave her to us to be our Mother as well (see John 19:26-27). Though racked with pain, He heard the thief on His right say, "Remember me, Lord, when you come into your kingdom." Jesus replied, "This day you will be with me in paradise" (Luke 23:43). These are the beautiful words all of us hope to hear one day.

Jesus not only suffered all this hardship and heartache on Calvary, but He then suffered even more. He not only emptied himself totally in body for us, even to shedding the last drop of His blood, but He also emptied himself totally in soul for us. Near the end, nearly blind and breathless from the torture, He suddenly felt completely abandoned by the Father. The feeling was so intense and wretched that He cried out, "My God, my God, why have you forsaken me?" (Matthew 27:46, Mark 15:34). In this suffering of soul, far greater than all His terrible physical suffering, He drank the last bitter dregs of His chalice of pain. He could do no more. He said, "It is finished" (John 20:30). And He said, "Father, into your hands I give my spirit" (Luke 23:46). He had no more to give. He had given all for love of us. And He died.

Prayer

O Jesus, on the cross, I weep at Your suffering and I weep for my sins because I know they have caused Your horrible pain. I see Your bloody body and thorn-crowned head, and I hang my head in shame. I am so sorry for having offended You. I regret so much my wayward ways.

Your dear and Sacred Heart is pierced, and blood flows out and then water (see John 19:34). You have no more to give for love of me. Please help me to love You more. Help me to be more appreciative of all You have done for me. Please help me to be like Your Mother, standing there beneath the cross, sad beyond tears, loyal and true to You in the end. That is my prayer. May I be the same, loyal and true to You to the end.

Lord, strengthen me, protect me. I want to be Your child, but You must help me. I can do nothing by myself. I thank You, dear Jesus, for giving Your life on the cross to save me from my sins and my foolishness. You know that I love You; help me to love You more. And grant on my last day that I may hear Your wonderful words addressed to the good thief, "This day you will be with me in paradise."

With an everlasting love, Lord, You have loved me; with overwhelming tenderness You embrace me. Help me to love You more and more. Amen.

Holy Saturday

Reflection

This was the most desolate day in Christianity. Christ had died and was buried. The great dream of a kingdom of love was gone; at least that is what the Apostles thought. The magnificent message of Jesus was shattered. Hatred had triumphed. All was lost. Gloom bordering on despair filled the hearts of the Apostles. They were so sad they could not speak. And at the same time they were dreadfully fearful that the authorities would come and take them and put them in prison or even put them to death as they had done to Jesus.

Jesus more than once had told the Apostles that His death would not be the end. But these men were slow learners; they had a difficult time understanding Jesus. His wonderful personality drew them to Him, but they rarely comprehended what He said. They were, in fact, the last to believe in the Resurrection. And Thomas was so hardheaded that he would not even believe when all the others said, "We have seen the Lord" (John 20:25).

The day Jesus was in the tomb was the lowest day ever in the lives of His followers. But then, the next day, everything changed. Jesus triumphed over death; the defeat of Good Friday became the victory of Easter, and night turned into day for the Apostles.

Jesus in the Resurrection showed that evil could not destroy goodness. The empty tomb revealed that love is stronger than anything, stronger even than death. Hatred had had its day, jealousy had done its worst, but now they were vanquished by the Risen Christ. The despondency of

His followers turned into an unutterable, unearthly joy.

The Resurrection demonstrated conclusively that Jesus was unlike any other human, that He was in truth what He had said He was, the spokesman for God in the world; more, He was the very Son of God sent from on high to redeem man and lead him back to God.

The Resurrection proved the truth of His great words, "All power in heaven and on earth has been given to me" (Matthew 28:18; see Luke 10:22).

The pettiness and legalism of the narrow-minded, small-hearted Pharisees was superseded by a love larger than life.

In the Resurrection Jesus in glory lets us see what it is like to live with God and what it will be like for us, His followers, after death.

No wonder on Easter Sunday we cry out, "Alleluia! Alleluia!" Christianity is joy, and Easter has made it so.

Prayer

This day, dear Lord, we wait for tomorrow. Unlike the Apostles, however, we know that Easter is a day of joy, that You rose in triumph, victorious over death and sin. And so, though we wait, we rejoice and give thanks to God for the glory of Easter. Our hearts are happy as we await You, the Risen Christ. We honor and praise You, and are grateful for all You have done for us. Our hearts say to us, "The earth is full of the goodness of the Lord [see Psalm 24:1]; sing to the Lord, for he has done marvelous deeds" (see Psalm 98:1). Your saving power, dear Jesus, is our glory. "Shout joyfully to God, all the earth" (Psalm 66:1).

Lent is over; Easter is here. May this holy season have been a time of blessings for me. May I rededicate myself to You. May Your saving graces come to me so that I may show Your love in all that I do. Be with me, Jesus; be with me and I am not afraid. Be with me, Jesus, and I can be Your instrument of love in the world. This is my prayer. Amen.

Lent with the Gospels:
A Biblical Suggestion

St. Francis de Sales reminds us that in our spiritual life we must be practical. We must act and not just dream. St. Ignatius Loyola called his meditations the "Spiritual Exercises." Just as the body needs exercise, so does the soul. We know how to exercise the body. What exercise should a person do to build up his soul? Perhaps something that happened to me at the time of my ordination, many years ago, might help.

When I was ordained, the bishop of our diocese generally had the ordination ceremony in the young man's home parish. My hometown was small, so our family went around asking people, Protestants and Catholics alike, if they would be kind enough to take in a guest or several guests for the ordination, since many relatives and friends were coming. Everyone agreed.

After the ordination and my First Mass, I went to the homes of all these people to thank them for their hospitality and generosity. I went up on the porch of a Protestant woman who had been especially kind. It was a warm day, and her door was open. As I knocked, I could see through the screen door that she was sitting in her living room reading a book. She came to the door, bringing the book, and I thanked her. We visited, and then by chance we both glanced at her book at the same time. It was the

II

Provisions
for the Trip

*Scriptures, Prayers
and Ideas to Ponder*

Bible. She explained, "Every morning on weekdays at ten o'clock, when it is quiet in the house, I sit down for 15 minutes and pray and read the Gospel."

As I say, that happened a long time ago, but I will never forget how inspired I was with her daily spiritual exercises. Wouldn't it be wonderful if you followed her example this Lent?

Besides daily prayer, one can add the daily devotion of Gospel reading. Following are suggestions for the daily reading of the Gospel of St. Mark during the weekdays of Lent, with excerpts from St. Matthew's account of the Passion for Holy Thursday and Good Friday. A person can read the suggested verses of the Gospel and then sit and think about what Jesus said and did. Remember: in the Gospel, our Lord is speaking to us.

Ash Wednesday: Mark, Ch. 1: vs. 1-20

Thursday after Ash Wednesday: Mark 1:21-45

Friday after Ash Wednesday: Mark 2:1-17

Monday, First Week of Lent: Mark 2:18-28

Tuesday, First Week of Lent: Mark 3:1-19

Wednesday, First Week of Lent: Mark 3:20-35

Thursday, First Week of Lent: Mark 4:1-20

Friday, First Week of Lent: Mark 4:21-41

Monday, Second Week of Lent: Mark 5:1-20

Tuesday, Second Week of Lent: Mark 5:21-43

Wednesday, Second Week of Lent: Mark 6:1-13

Thursday, Second Week of Lent: Mark 6:14-29

Friday, Second Week of Lent: Mark 6:30-56

Monday, Third Week of Lent: Mark 7:1-23

Tuesday, Third Week of Lent: Mark 7:24-37

Wednesday, Third Week of Lent: Mark 8:1-38

Thursday, Third Week of Lent: Mark 9:1-29

Friday, Third Week of Lent: Mark 9:30-50
Monday, Fourth Week of Lent: Mark 10:1-16
Tuesday, Fourth Week of Lent: Mark 10:17-31
Wednesday, Fourth Week of Lent: Mark 10:32-52
Thursday, Fourth Week of Lent: Mark 11:1-19
Friday, Fourth Week of Lent: Mark 11:20-33
Monday, Fifth Week of Lent: Mark 12:1-17
Tuesday, Fifth Week of Lent: Mark 12:18-34
Wednesday, Fifth Week of Lent: Mark 12:35-44
Thursday, Fifth Week of Lent: Mark 13:1-36
Friday, Fifth Week of Lent: Mark 14:1-42
Monday of Holy Week: Mark 14:43-72
Tuesday of Holy Week: Mark 15:1-20
Wednesday of Holy Week: Mark 15:21-47
Holy Thursday: Matthew Ch. 26: vs. 14-46
Good Friday: Matthew 27:1-2, 11-50

(If you follow this plan and wish to do Gospel reading on the weekends, you can choose your own text — maybe the Acts of the Apostles, which will follow our Lord's disciples putting the Gospel into action; it is such an exciting story that you might find yourself reading two chapters or so at a time. — R.M.)

In the next Lenten season, one might take up the Gospel of St. John — a slightly longer narrative, but one that is rich in characterization of the Apostles and proofs of the divinity of Jesus — finishing with the Passion according to St. Luke:

Ash Wednesday: John, Ch. 1: vs. 1-28
Tuesday after Ash Wednesday: John 1:29-51
Wednesday after Ash Wednesday: John 2:1-23
Thursday after Ash Wednesday: John 3:1-36
Friday after Ash Wednesday: John 4:1-38

Monday, First Week of Lent: John 4:39-5:9
Tuesday, First Week of Lent: John 5:10-46
Wednesday, First Week of Lent: John 6:1-40
Thursday, First Week of Lent: John 6:41-71
Friday, First Week of Lent: John 7:1-24
Monday, Second Week of Lent: John 7:25-8:1
Tuesday, Second Week of Lent: John 8:2-30
Wednesday, Second Week of Lent: John 8:31-59
Thursday, Second Week of Lent: John 9:1-34
Friday, Second Week of Lent: John 9:35-10:21
Monday, Third Week of Lent: John 10:22-42
Tuesday, Third Week of Lent: John 11:1-44
Wednesday, Third Week of Lent: John 11:44-12:11
Thursday, Third Week of Lent: John 12:12-36
Friday, Third Week of Lent: John 12:37-50
Monday, Fourth Week of Lent: John 13:1-30
Tuesday, Fourth Week of Lent: John 13:31-14:24
Wednesday, Fourth Week of Lent: John 14:25-15:27
Thursday, Fourth Week of Lent: John 16:1-33
Friday, Fourth Week of Lent: John 17:1-27
Monday, Fifth Week of Lent: John 18:1-27
Tuesday, Fifth Week of Lent: John 18:28-19:11
Wednesday, Fifth Week of Lent: John 19:12-30
Thursday, Fifth Week of Lent: John 19:31-42
Friday, Fifth Week of Lent: John 20:1-18
Monday of Holy Week: John 20:19-31
Tuesday of Holy Week: John 21:1-14
Wednesday of Holy Week: John 21:15-25
Holy Thursday: Luke Ch. 22: vs. 1-53
Good Friday: Luke 22:54-23:49

Again, if you follow this plan and wish to supplement it, weekend readings could be your own choice. You might sample the New Testament Epistles; they are a great source of Christian teaching and devotion — from the letters of St. Paul to those of Ss. Peter, James, John and Jude.)

A third Lenten cycle of Gospel reading could take up the Gospel of St. Matthew, ending in Holy Week with St. John's account of the Passion. Since St. Matthew's Gospel is longer, weekend readings are suggested:

Ash Wednesday: Matthew, Ch. 1: vs. 1-25
Thursday after Ash Wednesday: Matthew 2:1-23
Friday after Ash Wednesday: Matthew 3:1-17
Saturday after Ash Wednesday: Matthew 4:1-22
First Sunday of Lent: Matthew 4:23-5:16
Monday, First Week of Lent: Matthew 5:17-48
Tuesday, First Week of Lent: Matthew 6:1-23
Wednesday, First Week of Lent: Matthew 6:24-7:12
Thursday, First Week of Lent: Matthew 7:13-8:4
Friday, First Week of Lent: Matthew 8:5-27
Saturday, First Week of Lent: Matthew 8:28-9:13
Second Sunday of Lent: Matthew 9:14-34
Monday, Second Week of Lent: Matthew 9:35-10:23
Tuesday, Second Week of Lent: Matthew 10:24-11:1
Wednesday, Second Week of Lent: Matthew 11:2-24
Thursday, Second Week of Lent: Matthew 11:25-12:21
Friday, Second Week of Lent: Matthew 12:22-45
Saturday, Second Week of Lent: Matthew 12:46-13:17
Third Sunday of Lent: Matthew 13:18-43
Monday, Third Week of Lent: Matthew 13:44-14:21
Tuesday, Third Week of Lent: Matthew 14:22-15:9
Wednesday, Third Week of Lent: Matthew 15:10-39
Thursday, Third Week of Lent: Matthew 16:1-28
Friday, Third Week of Lent: Matthew 17:1-23
Saturday, Third Week of Lent: Matthew 17:24-18:20

Fourth Sunday of Lent: Matthew 18:21-19:2
Monday, Fourth Week of Lent: Matthew 19:3-30
Tuesday, Fourth Week of Lent: Matthew 20:1-28
Wednesday, Fourth Week of Lent: Matthew
 20:29-21:17
Thursday, Fourth Week of Lent: Matthew 21:18-45
Friday, Fourth Week of Lent: Matthew 22:1-22
Saturday, Fourth Week of Lent: Matthew 22:23-33
Fifth Sunday of Lent: Matthew 22:34-46
Monday, Fifth Week of Lent: Matthew 23:1-39
Tuesday, Fifth Week of Lent: Matthew 24:1-51
Wednesday, Fifth Week of Lent: Matthew 25:1-30
Thursday, Fifth Week of Lent: Matthew 25:31-26:5
Friday, Fifth Week of Lent: Matthew 26:6-35
Saturday, Fifth Week of Lent: Matthew 26:36-56
Palm Sunday: Matthew 26:57-75
Monday of Holy Week: Matthew 27:1-31
Tuesday of Holy Week: Matthew 27:32-66
Wednesday of Holy Week: Matthew 28:1-20
Holy Thursday: John 13:1-38, 18:1-11
Good Friday: John 18:12-19:37

Finally, if you spend the next Lent reading through the Gospel of St. Luke (including weekends if possible, since this is the longest Gospel) and finish with the Passion according to St. Mark, you will have reflected on all four Gospels in four successive Lents:

Ash Wednesday: Luke, Ch. 1: vs. 1-38
Thursday after Ash Wednesday: Luke 1:39-80
Friday after Ash Wednesday: Luke 2:1-21
Saturday after Ash Wednesday: Luke 2:21-52
First Sunday of Lent: Luke 3:1-22

Monday, First Week of Lent: Luke 3:23-4:13
Tuesday, First Week of Lent: Luke 4:14-44
Wednesday, First Week of Lent: Luke 5:1-26
Thursday, First Week of Lent: Luke 5:27-6:11
Friday, First Week of Lent: Luke 6:12-49
Saturday, First Week of Lent: Luke 7:1-35
Second Sunday of Lent: Luke 7:36-8:21
Monday, Second Week of Lent: Luke 8:22-56
Tuesday, Second Week of Lent: Luke 9:1-22
Wednesday, Second Week of Lent: Luke 9:23-50
Thursday, Second Week of Lent: Luke 9:51-10:20
Friday, Second Week of Lent: Luke 10:21-42
Saturday, Second Week of Lent: Luke 11:1-28
Third Sunday of Lent: Luke 11:29-54
Monday, Third Week of Lent: Luke 12:1-34
Tuesday, Third Week of Lent: Luke 12:35-59
Wednesday, Third Week of Lent: Luke 13:1-30
Thursday, Third Week of Lent: Luke 13:31-14:24
Friday, Third Week of Lent: Luke 14:25-15:10
Saturday, Third Week of Lent: Luke 15:11-32
Fourth Sunday of Lent: Luke 16:1-31
Monday, Fourth Week of Lent: Luke 17:1-37
Tuesday, Fourth Week of Lent: Luke 18:1-30
Wednesday, Fourth Week of Lent: Luke 18:31-19:10
Thursday, Fourth Week of Lent: Luke 19:11-40
Friday, Fourth Week of Lent: Luke 19:41-20:8
Saturday, Fourth Week of Lent: Luke 20:9-18
Fifth Sunday of Lent: Luke 20:19-47
Monday, Fifth Week of Lent: Luke 21:1-19
Tuesday, Fifth Week of Lent: Luke 21:20-38
Wednesday, Fifth Week of Lent: Luke 22:1-23
Thursday, Fifth Week of Lent: Luke 22:24-46
Friday, Fifth Week of Lent: Luke 22:47-62

Saturday, Fifth Week of Lent: Luke 22:63-23:12
Palm Sunday: Luke 23:13-31
Monday of Holy Week: Luke 23:32-49
Tuesday of Holy Week: Luke 23:49-24:12
Wednesday of Holy Week: Luke 24:13-53
Holy Thursday: Mark 14:12-50
Good Friday: Mark 14:53-15:39

Starters for Your Own Reflections

Sometimes, even after reading a chapter of Holy Scripture, reflection comes hard. The mind may still not be calm enough to concentrate on the Gospel message, or maybe the Lord's message is so rich in meaning that it is difficult to zero in on one train of thought.

Over the years I have collected the following 57 "Points to Ponder" from various sources. You might call them "Myers' 57 Varieties" — brief statements of great truths from a variety of people, many of them saints, perhaps a few sinners, mostly Christian writers, poets and commentators.

It should take no more than one or two of these epigrams — *pensées*, as they were called by Blaise Pascal — to start your spirit in motion toward sincere and fervent prayer.

Points to Ponder

Christ came to do His Father's will. If anyone among the sons of men might have allowably taken his own pleasure and have done his own will, it was our Lord. Yet He said, "In truth, I come to do Thy will, O God." And St.

Paul said, "Christ pleased not himself." He thought not of himself but offered himself up to God for us.

— Cardinal Newman

When you begin to be infinitely wicked and God ceases to be infinitely merciful, then you can begin to despair.

— Archbishop Fulton Sheen

It is impossible to think of any individual who has ever contributed or ever will contribute as much service toward the reconciliation of men with God as Mary.

— Pope Leo XIII

I don't care what happens to me — God will direct my life.

— St. Francis of Assisi

With the sacraments, Christ feeds His people, and by them the soul is strengthened.

— St. Ambrose

Pray that you will gain the great gift of perseverance.

— Thomas Merton

We need to pray to calm and compose the inner self.

— Louis Evely

Suffering purifies the soul.

— Abbé Courtois

At the Last Supper Our Lord instituted a ceremony which He wanted observed as the form of worship of His followers: today we call this reenactment of the Last Supper the Mass.

— Monsignor Ronald Knox

Prayer is a searching for God — and resting in Him.

— Thomas Merton

In Holy Communion at Mass we quench our tepidity with the Love that inflames us.

— Gerald Vann

Our faith is identical with that of the early Christians.

— Thomas Aquinas

We are in God's hands — or nowhere.

— W.H. Auden

In the opinion there is a God, there are difficulties; but in the contrary opinion there are absurdities.

— Voltaire

Our intellect stammers and boggles when it tries to reach the divine. Anything we can think of is a pale reflection of the Creator. The things we see and touch on this earth are only the shadows cast by the Maker.

— Monsignor Ronald Knox

Our joy comes from God who is our home.

— William Wordsworth

God hates nothing He has made.

— Thomas Merton

It is not likely that the heavenly Father is less loving than an earthly father.

— Michel Quoist

God does not want the forced obedience of slaves. Instead He covets our voluntary love.

— Catherine Marshall

We are not sent into this world for nothing; everyone who breathes, high and low, has a work. God sees every one of us, and He created each of us for a purpose.

— Cardinal Newman

Did not Our Lord say that He would never reject anyone who came to Him? "He who comes to me, I will not cast out," He said.

— Archbishop Fulton Sheen

God's tabernacle on earth is the Church.

— St. Augustine

To those who love God, all things work together unto good.

— St. Paul

I know nothing of tomorrow but that the love of God will rise before the sun.

— Boussuet

Lift up your eyes and see all the things God has made in beauty.

— St. Francis of Assisi

We can be so preoccupied with the works of God that we forget the God of works.

— Pope John Paul II

The deepest prayer is a surrender to God, and daily prayer is a purification and preparation for that.

— Thomas Merton

The Church lives again the life of Christ.

— Christopher Dawson

It is the peculiar property of the Church that when she is buffeted, she triumphs.

— St. Hilary

God loves us, every one, as though there were but one of us to love.

— St. Augustine

There are only two classes of people in the world: those who fall down and stay down, and those who fall down and get back up again. Count your resurrections as well as your falls.

— Archbishop Fulton Sheen

Whoever seeks the truth seeks God.

— Thomas Merton

Though things are difficult, do not feel sad. We are not alone. God, our good Father, is with us, so why should we be afraid?

— St. Francis of Assisi

We would have to do ourselves violence not to believe in God.

— Charles Péguy

A God we could comprehend fully would be no God at all.

— Hilda Graef

God is waiting to love man through us.

— Michel Quoist

God loves us more than a mother can love her child.

— Charles de Foucauld

I see the figure of this man after the scourging. Jesus is thirty but he now looks sixty, for he bears all our burdens. His eyes rivet me and move my heart to great pity.

— Cardinal Newman

This Jesus whom you crucified — there is salvation in no other.

— St. Peter

Kneeling before the tabernacle and praying means more to the people than all the discussions of dogmas.

— Bernard Häring

Religion gives a person an anchor in life — something to tie to.

— Harry Reasoner

Religion is the only thing that makes sense of life.

— Hugh Walpole

God will make himself known to those who seek Him sincerely.

— Pascal

Some men still trace the greater from the less and strive to account for the soul from flesh, dreams from dust, striving to extract a plus from a minus.

— Alfred Noyes

It would be easier for a printing plant to blow up and all the pieces of print to come down and print the dictionary than for the world to be explained without a creator.

— Edwin Grant Conklin

Christ does not ask all, only a few saints, to be crucified with Him — but He asks all to be little children.

— Thomas Merton

Everything best, beautiful, most desirable, money cannot buy.

— Hermann Hesse

God seeks to inspire us to be creative.

— Archbishop Anthony Bloom

Man is miserable until he partakes of God.

— Cardinal Newman

Christ pleased not himself.

— St. Paul

When God came to earth He healed man. Jesus accepted the company of people whose company others didn't want. In giving ourselves to Christ we only give up our pettiness.

— Archbishop Anthony Bloom

Only by Christ is the mind strengthened to resist the perpetually changing mood of modern man.

— G.K. Chesterton

God reconciled and renewed His rebel world through Christ.

— Monsignor Ronald Knox

Mary is the Mother of all living, hope for the weak, refuge for sinners, comforter of the afflicted. We kiss the hem of her garment and kneel in the shadow of her throne. For she, O gracious Lady, is full of grace and glory.

— Cardinal Newman

Do not think of God as always looking around corners to jot down your sins. He is always looking at your good deeds, seeing every drink of cold water you give in His name, every time you visit the sick, every small act of kindness, every time you are pleasant with your family when you don't feel like it.

— Archbishop Fulton Sheen

In prayer it is more important to love much than to think much.

— St. Teresa of Avila

Let nothing disturb you, nothing affright you, all things are passing, God never changes; patient endurance attains to all things; who God possesses is wanting in nothing; God alone is enough.

— St. Thérèse of Lisieux

Prayers of the Saints:
A Road Map for Prayer

The prayers written down in the first section of this book are not meant to be recited by rote. They are a natural outgrowth of the reflections they follow, meant only as a pattern for your own reflections and prayers.

When you read and reflect on the Gospels, you should be moved to form your own mental prayer, in your own words or without any words at all, with sentiments of strengthened faith, hope, love and sorrow for sin.

The following 22 examples of prayer are from the greatest students of prayer the world has ever known — the saints of God. Again, they are only meant as models — a road map, if you will, for your own conversations with the Lord. See how they are moved to praise God and His Blessed Mother, and what they ask for in their petitions.

O God, give us Your love, since You know how much we need it.

— St. Teresa of Avila

O Lord, my good times and hard times, my work and my leisure, my life and my death, in good health and sickness — I offer all to You. Teach me through the Holy Spirit how best to live. By Your holy graces help me to be patient, to help people with unfailing sympathy, and with wisdom. Let me learn how to comfort others in their sadness, strengthen them in their weakness, lift them up when they fall. Make me, Lord, to feel with them in sickness, to understand their complaining, to comfort them in sorrow.

— St. Aelred

What return shall we make to God for all He has done for us? He has been so generous. He has given us all good things, even though we are sinners. How can we repay His blessings? Let us strive to pray and grow in love so that we can serve Him better. We are lost if we do not love.

— St. Paulinus of Nola

O great and admirable Jesus, the angels do not deem themselves worthy to look upon You, but You desire me to receive You into my heart in Holy Communion. O Lord, how good You are. How is it possible that the King of heaven and earth would deign to take His abode in me, who am full of imperfection and sin? And in coming to me He transforms me into a paradise of grace and blessings. I am unworthy but I am so grateful.

— St. John Eudes

O God, forgive my sins against You, forgive them all. You are good and You love all men. And I ask the prayers of Your most holy Mother and all the saints so that my sins may be taken away so that I can receive Your holy and immaculate Body and Your precious Blood for the healing of my soul and body; for Yours is the kingdom, the power and the glory, Father, Son and Holy Spirit, now and forever.

— St. John Chrysostom

Give me Yourself, O my God, give Yourself once more to me. Behold, I love You, and if my love is too weak a thing, grant me to love You more strongly. I know that my poor love falls short, but nonetheless let my soul hasten to Your embrace, O Lord. This only do I know, that it is not good for me when You are not with me, and all the riches in the world that are not my God are worthless.

— St. Augustine

No trial has come to me that I cannot gladly bear when I look at You, O Jesus, on the cross in agony. With so good a Friend, so good a Companion at our side, one who suffered so much for us, one can bear anything. He helps us; He gives us strength; He is our true Friend.

— St. Teresa of Avila

We give thanks to You, the kindly Giver of every good thing, God the Father of our Lord Jesus Christ and our Savior, for He himself protects us, helps us, and supports our being. In mercy He has made us His own. We beseech Him now to keep watch over us this day and all the days of our life. Give us Your peace, Lord, and keep us in Your peace, as You give us all things. Take possession of us now, O God our Savior, for we daily need Your help.

— Coptic Liturgy of St. Basil

Grant me, I beseech You, my God, in the name of Jesus Christ Your Son, the charity which never fails, that my light may shine, warming my own heart and enlightening others.

— St. Columbanus

Almighty, everlasting God, behold, I approach the Sacrament of Your only begotten Son, our Lord Jesus Christ, in the Holy Eucharist. I come to our Eucharistic Lord as a sick man to the physician who will save his life, as a man unclean to the fountain of mercy, as a blind man to the eternal light, one poor and needy to the Lord of heaven and earth; praying that in Your boundless generosity You will deign to cure my sickness, wash away my defilement, enlighten my blindness, enrich my poverty and clothe my nakedness.

— St. Thomas Aquinas

O Blessed Virgin Mary, who can adequately repay you and thank you for giving your wondrous assent to the angel, who brought Jesus to earth to rescue a fallen world? Accept our poor thanks and deep gratitude. We ask, Blessed Mother, that you pray for the remission of our sins. Help to obtain for us pardon from the Lord, for we are fearful and you are the hope of sinners. Holy Mary, aid the afflicted, lift up the fainthearted, comfort the sorrowful, pray for all the people, and especially may those who are needy feel your help and protection. Assist us, Blessed Mary, you who are wholly blessed and who merited to bear the Redeemer of the world.

— St. Augustine

I hope in You and Your promise to love us, O Lord. You are my dear Savior. I sincerely repent of all my offenses

against You. I love You, Lord, but I love You so little — I wish so much to love You more. Please help me.
— St. Alphonsus Liguori

O dearest Jesus, O most blessed Lord, my Savior and my consolation, thank You for the graces that You give me. Thank You for the Holy Eucharist wherein You lower yourself to my poor heart. I praise You and I adore You, and I thank You for Your goodness. Praised be Your mercy and Your love. O dear Jesus, my heart weeps for joy and my soul is stirred to happiness by Your kindness to me. You are my love, and it is Your love that frees me from harm. I go forth with firm confidence because the richness of Your blessings are with me.
— St. Gertrude

Soul of Christ, sanctify me; Body of Christ, save me; Blood of Christ, fill me; water from the side of Christ, wash me; passion of Christ, strengthen me; O good Jesus, hear me. Within Your wounds hide me; suffer me never to be separated from You; from the malicious enemy defend me; in the hour of my death call me; and bid me come unto You; that with the saints I may praise You, forever and ever. Amen.
— St. Ignatius Loyola

Too late have I loved You, O Beauty, so ancient and yet so new; late have I loved You. For behold You were with me, but I did not seek You; in my waywardness I rushed about heedlessly seeking the things of the world. You were with me but I was not with You. I was kept from the Creator by my fascination with Your creatures. But then You called me and cried to me and forced me to open my eyes. You sent forth Your light and showed me Your splendor and put to flight my blindness. You let Your fragrance fall upon me and I breathed it in and turned to You; I tasted You and now I hunger and thirst for You. You touched me and now I burn and yearn for You.

— St. Augustine

Divine Word, worthy of all admiraton and all love, You draw me continually toward yourself. You came down into this world of exile to suffer and die to bring souls to the bosom of the Father. And now, though You returned to heaven, where there is glory and light forever, You still frequent this valley of tears, hidden under the appearance of the Sacred Host. You are still ready to feed my soul which is so weak that it would sink back into nothingness at any second if You did not give me life at every moment. Jesus, You love me so fondly, and when I meet such fondness, how can my heart fail to go out to You, and how can my trust in You have any limits?

— St. Thérèse of the Child Jesus

Who, as you, O Lady, can render our often barren hearts fruitful and soften the coldness and callousness of our nature? Please implant in us the sacred seeds of holiness to stir up our flagging ways and make our work fruitful. We beseech you, dear Mother Mary, to give us grace to love more and show forth the winning ways of heaven.

— St. Hildefonsus

Pierce, O dear sweet Jesus, my inmost being with Your most joyous and wondrous love, with Your great and beautiful charity, so that my soul may ever languish and melt with love and longing for You. May I ever yearn for You and Your heavenly home, so that in death I may be dissolved and be with You forever. Grant that my soul may ever hunger for You. May my soul always thirst after You, the fountain of life, of wisdom and knowledge, of eternal light. May my whole being ever seek You and find You and meditate upon You and do all things for the praise and glory of Your name.

Help me to persevere to the end, dear Lord, with humility and love and peace and kindness. May You be my hope, my riches, my joy, my rest, my refreshment, my refuge, my wisdom, my treasure. In You may my mind and my heart be firmly rooted forever.

— St. Bonaventure

I give You thanks, O holy Lord, Father Almighty, Eternal God, who have granted, not for any merit of mine, but solely out of the goodness of Your mercy, to satisfy me, a sinner, Your unworthy servant, with the Precious Body and Blood of Your Son, our Lord Jesus Christ. I pray that this Holy Communion be a saving plea for me unto forgiveness. May it be for me an increase of faith and good will, an emptying out of my vices, the extinction of all concupiscence and lust, an increase of charity and patience, of humility and obedience, and of all virtues; a strong defense against the snares of all enemies, visible and invisible; the perfect quieting of all my evil impulses, both in body and spirit. May this Holy Communion be for me a firm cleaving to You, the one true God, and a pledge of a blessed destiny in heaven.

I ask You please, dear God, that You grant to me, a sinner, Your blessings so that I may participate in Your wondrous heavenly banquet, where You, with Your Son and the Holy Spirit, are for Your saints true light, the fullness of contentment, eternal joy, gladness without end and perfect bliss. I beg this through Christ, our Lord. Amen.

— St. Thomas Aquinas

Before Your eyes, O Lord, I bring my offenses and I compare them to the troubles I have had; if I consider the evil I have done, what I suffer is very little. Still, though I feel the punishment of sin, I withdraw not from the obstinacy of sinning. Though sin brings torment and grief, my proud and stubborn neck is not bent; though I groan because of my sins, I do not mend my ways.

If You spare me, Lord, I do not correct my deeds; if You punish me, I cannot endure it. I confess my wrongdoings, but after Your visitation I forget that I have wept. Grant then, O Almighty God, without my deserving it, the pardon I need and ask for; You who made us out of nothing can help us most of all.

— St. Augustine

Have mercy on me, O Lord, for I put my trust in You. I lift up my heart to You, dear Jesus; show me the way I should go. Into Your hands, Lord, I commit myself all through the day. I commend to You my family and loved ones, my friends, relatives, the needy, and the faithful departed. Keep us, O Lord; watch over us and protect us. Let Your Holy Spirit enlighten us and never let us be separated from You.

— St. Edmund of Canterbury

Do strengthen my soul, Good of all good, my Jesus, and let me do something for You, for no one could bear to receive as much as I have and pay nothing in return. Per-

mit me not to come to You at the end of this day with empty hands. Help me today to bring Your love into the world.
— St. Teresa of Avila

O blessed Jesus, let me deeply consider the greatness of Your love towards me. O blessed Jesus, give me the grace heartily to thank You for Your benefits. O sweet Jesus, possess my heart and hold it and keep it close to You.
— St. John Fisher

III

A Lenten Sojourn

Meditations and Devotions

A Road of Sorrows:
The Way of the Cross

Introduction

Jesus says to us:

Come with me now and walk beside me as I make my sorrowful journey through the streets of Jerusalem up to the hill of execution. Let us make this journey to Calvary together.

I was taken prisoner last night as I prayed in the Garden of Gethsemane. All the Apostles ran away. Earlier I had asked them to pray with me, but they fell asleep.

My heart was broken when I saw Judas, one of my chosen friends, leading the guards out to arrest me. He betrayed me with a kiss.

My heart was broken again when Peter denied that he knew me. It was difficult enough suffering at the hands of evil-minded men who beat me and crowned me with hideous thorns, and who ridiculed me and lied about me. There was not a shred of justice or truth at my trial. But it was even worse to be denied by my close friends.

Please do not you, my friend, also desert me. Come with me now as I climb the hill to Calvary. Follow me, dear friend; follow my bloody footsteps as I walk along up to the hill where I will suffer and die on the cross for love of you.

First Station

Pilate Condemns Jesus to Die

Jesus says to us:

Pilate decides I must die. He did not want to condemn me to death. He knew I was innocent. But he was a person who tried to please everyone and ended up pleasing no one, not even himself. Poor Pilate!

He proclaimed that I was not guilty, and then — the only person in Judea who could condemn me — he turned around and signed my death warrant. Truth was not honored on Good Friday. Pilate had wiggled and squirmed every way he knew how to get out of condemning me. But in the end, he was afraid of losing his job if he did the right thing, so he gave in. He then washed his hands before the people and proclaimed, "I am innocent of the blood of this just man." But next he told the soldiers to take me out and murder me.

So it is with people who want to be popular at all cost.

We respond:

Dear Jesus, I am so sorry for my sins that have made You make this sorrowful journey. Please forgive me, Lord. Please, please help me to overcome my sins and be more faithful to You.

(Our Father, etc.)

Second Station

Jesus Is Made to Carry His Cross

Jesus says to us:

Pilate proclaimed my innocence to the people, and then he handed me over to the soldiers to be executed. These barbarians, after beating me almost to death, put the heavy cross on my bloody shoulders. And then, kicking and pushing me, they pulled me along the torturous way to Calvary outside the city gates.

Look at me, my friend, and see what sin can do. Still, I love you so very much I will do anything for you.

We respond:

O dearest Jesus, I am so ashamed that the soldiers acted like animals and treated You so terribly. I am doubly ashamed because I know it is my sins that caused Your suffering.

Lord Jesus, I cannot look at Your bloody face; You endured all this for love of me. My heart is broken. I can only plead for Your grace and blessings.

(Our Father, etc.)

Third Station

Jesus Falls the First Time

Jesus says to us:
I am so weak I cannot take another step. I try — but I cannot. I have lost so much blood that I faint and fall to the hard cobblestone street, and the heavy cross comes crashing down upon my back, already bloody from the merciless beating of the soldiers.

I stagger to my feet again somehow. Now do you believe I love you more than words can tell? Now do you believe I love you so much I will do anything for you?

We respond:
I weep as I see You, dear Jesus, my dearest Friend, lying under the cross, flat on the ground, covered with blood so that it is hard to recognize You, kicked and pulled by the inhuman soldiers.

I weep and pledge that I will try harder to be more caring and kind to my neighbors, to make up for the brutality You suffered for me.

(Our Father, etc.)

Fourth Station

Jesus Meets His Afflicted Mother

Jesus says to us:

My Mother made her way through the crowd, and she stands there holding out her hands to help me — but the heartless soldiers push her back and will not let her come closer. Through my bloody eyes I can see the tears flowing down her cheeks. Her eyes are full of the most terrible sorrow. Her heart is broken. And just to see her, my dearest Mother, suffering so much broke my heart as well.

We respond:

Dear Mother Mary, pray for me. O sorrowful Mother, come to my assistance as you tried to assist your Son. Mother in heaven, bless me and give me strength and courage. You had such courage. The Apostles all ran away, but you stayed with Jesus. Help me to be loyal to Him, just as you were, faithful and true to the very end.

(Our Father, etc.)

Fifth Station

Simon Helps Jesus to Carry His Cross

Jesus says to us:

I was so weak I could hardly walk. The soldiers did not want me to die on the way to my crucifixion; it would have spoiled their fun. And so they grabbed a man in the crowd, Simon of Cyrene, and forced him to help me carry my cross.

I made this sorrowful journey for you, my dear friend, to save you from sin and to gain for you the graces that will help you enter into eternal life and the joy of heaven.

We respond:

Thank you for Your generous and gracious kindness, dear Lord. I can never thank You enough. Help me, please, to be more grateful. And, Jesus, please help me to carry my cross in life, as You permitted Simon to help You with Yours.

(Our Father, etc.)

Sixth Station

Veronica Wipes the Face of Jesus

Jesus says to us:

Blood has covered my face so that I cannot see, and I stumble along. The thorns pierce my head and cause horrible pain at every unsteady step. Then I feel someone wiping my face, and when I can see again I bless this loving woman for her gentle kindness. Amid the brutish, cruel, cursing soldiers, she is like a ray of light in the darkness, like a cool, refreshing breeze on a hot, muggy afternoon.

We respond:

Dear Jesus, though Peter denied You and Judas betrayed You, it was Veronica who showed You that there was still kindness in the world. May her graciousness be an example for me. There was such sadness on Your way of the cross, but a woman with an act of love for a few moments turned the darkness into light. May I do the same. There are many people around me in distress who need a gesture of graciousness. Help me to see those in need, and inspire me, like Veronica, to help them.

(Our Father, etc.)

Seventh Station

Jesus Falls the Second Time

Jesus says to us:
I collapse to the street once more. But I rise again. May this help you, dear friend, to take heart when you fall. If in my bloody agony, so near death, I can rise up again — so can you rise up after you have fallen. I teach you to hold on, not to give up. Never, never give up. I will always be beside you when you fall to help you up again. Do not be discouraged. I am with you. And in this sorrowful journey you see how much I love you.

We respond:
Lord Jesus, how often I feel like giving up. Especially then do I need Your blessings. Let me then remember You crushed beneath the cross, suffering beyond belief, and yet You struggle to Your feet once more.

I cannot give up when I think of You. But I cannot get up without Your help. You have promised, though, that You will always be there to help me. I believe this. I know You will.

(Our Father, etc.)

Eighth Station

Jesus Meets the Weeping Women

Jesus says to us:

As I near the top of the hill, some women with their children stand beside the road weeping for me. I turn and bless them. I am grateful for their compassion. Even though I can hardly see, I offer them words of comfort.

Dear friend, I also have words of comfort for you, if you ask for them. I have many blessings for you, as well, if you seek me out. As you show kindness to others, I will show kindness to you.

We respond:

Good and gentle Jesus, I am amazed that even in Your agony You think of others. Help me to be more like You, more thoughtful, more courteous, more considerate and gracious.

I am often so selfish. If I have a little pain I collapse in self-pity. Let me look at You with Your compassion on this terrible journey, and let me imitate Your kindness.

(Our Father, etc.)

Ninth Station

Jesus Falls the Third Time

Jesus says to us:

I have come to the place of execution. I have climbed the hill and now I fall, here where ignorant, inhuman men will murder me — and for what? Because I blessed and helped and healed people; because I taught them of the love of God. Is this a crime?

I am so exhausted, completely and totally exhausted, that I cannot go on.

We respond:

Jesus, Lord, help me to accept my cross and not complain so much. Help me to offer up my troubles as a prayer and unite them with Your great suffering for the sake of souls.

O Jesus, I am sometimes angry. Let me look at Your superhuman patience and be more calm and resigned. Make me less restless; let me rest in Your arms. Give me Your peace of mind; give me Your grace or I will surely fall again, but with You and Your help I can carry on.

(Our Father, etc.)

Tenth Station

Jesus Is Stripped of His Garments

Jesus says to us:

On the hill of Calvary, before the jeering mob, the soldiers brutally pull off my bloody robe so roughly that the skin comes with it. Diabolically, they sneer and ridicule me in my humiliation. I offer all this to the Father.

Dearest friend, see how I love you. I will endure anything for love of you. Will you not love me a little in return?

We respond:

Jesus, You are so willing to accept every suffering and humiliation for me. But I, in my turn, am so proud, and pride ruins everything. Grant me a little of Your humility, for humility is the secret of the saints; humility is the beginning of true wisdom. I beg You, Lord Jesus, to bless me so that I can strip myself of my pride and with humility love and serve You more.

(Our Father, etc.)

Eleventh Station

Jesus Is Nailed to the Cross

Jesus says to us:

The soldiers, with cruelty unknown to animals, throw me on the wood of the cross and with great hammers nail the huge spikes into my hands and feet. Every blow sends pain to every part of my body. I cannot endure it — but I do endure it. I endure it for love of you. I want to save you from sin and make it possible for you to gain paradise. And so I accept this suffering; I extend my arms on the cross to welcome you with all my heart.

We respond:

O Sacred Heart of Jesus, Your love is so great and my love is so weak. I look to You, Lord, with arms extended on the cross, willingly enduring all for love of me. I beg for Your help. You know I can do nothing without You. In my weakness, like a small child, I cry out to You. O crucified Christ, I beg Your blessings and the graces You won for me by enduring this horrible ordeal.

(Our Father, etc.)

Twelfth Station

Jesus Dies on the Cross

Jesus says to us:

I cried out from the cross, "I thirst." They brought me wine, but I refused it. Mine was not a physical thirst but a spiritual thirst. I thirst for souls. I thirst for your soul, dear friend. See my suffering and agony on the cross for love of you. The pain is so intense I can hardly endure it; my face is covered with blood; my every muscle is on fire with pain. See how I love you.

Won't you suffer a little for the sake of your soul? I suffered all this for you; won't you strive to accept your pain to purify your heart? Self-discipline and penance are the way to control yourself. You complain that you sin, but what do you do to try not to sin? If you practice penance you will grow strong in soul and fortify your will against weakness. However, only you can do penance for yourself; no one can do it for you.

We respond:

I look at the crucifix and I do not know what to say. I hang my head in shame for my sins. All this great pain that You, O Lord, suffered to save me, and I do so little for myself. Give me courage, dear Christ. I am determined through prayer and self-discipline to become a better, stronger person, as You, Jesus, want me to be.

(Our Father, etc.)

Thirteenth Station

Jesus Is Taken Down From the Cross

Jesus says to us:

My lifeless body is laid in the arms of my poor Mother — and her heart is broken. No words can express her sorrow and suffering. Just look at her sadness and your heart will be broken too.

We respond:

Dearest Mary, my Mother, my heart goes out to you in your great sorrow. I cannot begin to imagine the suffering this caused you — the lifeless body of your dearest, cherished Son in your arms. This was the greatest tragedy of your life. And yet you continue to be brave, showing an unearthly courage.

Blessed Mary, you are my Mother. I look to you and ask that you will bless me so that I may be a little more like your Son. That is what you wish for me, Mother, more than anything else. And I know you will help me. Aren't mothers always there when you need them?

(Hail Mary, etc.)

Fourteenth Station

Jesus Is Placed in the Tomb

Jesus says to us:

My dear Mother arranges my body with her own hands. Tears are running down her cheeks. She who was the first to take me in her arms, at my birth in the cave at Bethlehem, is now the last to arrange my body for burial.

Yet she has the greatest faith and courage. Of all those there at the tomb, she, with unwavering hope, is the only one who believes that this is not the end. She alone has confidence in her heart that I will rise again, as I promised.

We respond:

I am grateful, dear Mary, for the magnificent faith you had. Please, Mother, help me to increase my faith and my hope and love. Please help me to be more like your Son in loving others.

Bless me, O Mary, that I may trust in God as you trusted in Him at this darkest time. When I am troubled or in pain, let me be like you in your tragic hour and put all my faith in God.

(Hail Mary, etc.)

Concluding Prayer

O Lord Jesus, Good Friday gave way to Easter Sunday. The sorrow and suffering of Calvary is not the last chapter in the book of Christianity. It is only an episode, as our suffering is only an episode in our lives. There is more. There is the empty tomb of Easter and joy. Christ is risen, alleluia! The crucifixion is important, but the resurrection is more important. Our faith is not centered on Your dying on the cross; our faith is centered on the Risen Christ. We are Easter people, so let us rejoice.

Christianity has a happy ending, and Christianity, because of Easter, is joy. Easter means to us what it meant to the Apostles, that Jesus is with us and will never leave us again. If that is not cause for rejoicing, then nothing in this life is. We are not alone; Christ walks with us, always and everywhere, until we go home and are with Him forever in heaven. As St. Paul tells us, "Rejoice . . . again I say, rejoice!" (Philippians 4:4). The Christian heart is a joyful heart, now and forever, because of Christ and because of the Resurrection.

The Resurrection tells us that we, with Christ, will rise again and live with Him in the glorious, heavenly kingdom of God.

For this we pray, O Lord. Amen.

A Lenten Psalter
(Selected Psalms)

Psalm 6

O Lord, rebuke me not in thy anger,
   nor chasten me in thy wrath.
Be gracious to me, O Lord, for I am languishing;
   O Lord, heal me, for my bones are troubled.
My soul also is sorely troubled.
   But thou, O Lord — how long?

Turn, O Lord, save my life;
   deliver me for the sake of thy steadfast love.
For in death there is no remembrance of thee;
   in Sheol who can give thee praise?

I am weary with my moaning;
   every night I flood my bed with tears;
   I drench my couch with my weeping.
My eye wastes away because of grief,
   it grows weak because of all my foes.

Depart from me, all you workers of evil;
   for the Lord has heard the sound of my weeping.
The Lord has heard my supplication;

the Lord accepts my prayer.
All my enemies shall be ashamed and sorely troubled;
   they shall turn back, and be put to shame in a moment.

Psalm 13(12)

How long, O Lord? Wilt thou forget me for ever?
   How long wilt thou hide thy face from me?
How long must I bear pain in my soul,
   and have sorrow in my heart all the day?
How long shall my enemy be exalted over me?

Consider and answer me, O Lord my God;
   lighten my eyes, lest I sleep the sleep of death;
lest my enemy say, "I have prevailed over him";
   lest my foes rejoice because I am shaken.

But I have trusted in thy steadfast love;
   my heart shall rejoice in thy salvation.
I will sing to the Lord, because he has dealt bountifully
     with me.

Psalm 22 (21)

My God, my God, why hast thou forsaken me?
   Why art thou so far from helping me, from the words of
     my groaning?

O my God, I cry by day, but thou dost not answer;
　　and by night, but find no rest.

Yet thou art holy,
　　enthroned on the praises of Israel.
In thee our fathers trusted;
　　they trusted, and thou didst deliver them.
To thee they cried and were saved;
　　in thee they trusted, and were not disappointed.

But I am a worm, and no man;
　　scorned by men, and despised by the people.
All who see me mock at me,
　　they make mouths at me, they wag their heads;
"He committed his cause to the Lord; let him deliver him,
　　let him rescue him, for he delights in him!"

Yet thou art he who took me from the womb;
　　thou didst keep me safe upon my mother's breasts.
Upon thee was I cast from my birth,
　　and since my mother bore me thou hast been my God.
Be not far from me,
　　for trouble is near
　　and there is none to help.

Many bulls encompass me,
　　strong bulls of Bashan surround me;
they open wide their mouths at me,
　　like a ravening and roaring lion.

I am poured out like water,
　　and all my bones are out of joint;
my heart is like wax,

it is melted within my breast;
my strength is dried up like a potsherd,
   and my tongue cleaves to my jaws;
   thou dost lay me in the dust of death.

Yea, dogs are round about me;
   a company of evildoers encircle me;
   they have pierced my hands and feet —
I can count all my bones —
   they stare and gloat over me;
they divide my garments among them,
   and for my raiment they cast lots.

But thou, O Lord, be not far off!
   O thou my help, hasten to my aid!
Deliver my soul from the sword,
   my life from the power of the dog!
Save me from the mouth of the lion,
   my afflicted soul from the horns of the wild oxen!

I will tell of thy name to my brethren;
   in the midst of the congregation I will praise thee:
You who fear the Lord, praise him!
   all you sons of Jacob, glorify him,
   and stand in awe of him, all you sons of Israel!
For he has not despised or abhorred
   the affliction of the afflicted;
and he has not hid his face from him,
   but has heard, when he cried to him.

From thee comes my praise in the great congregation;
   my vows I will pay before those who fear him.
The afflicted shall eat and be satisfied;

those who seek him shall praise the Lord!
May your hearts live for ever!

All the ends of the earth shall remember
and turn to the Lord;
and all the families of the nations
shall worship before him.
For dominion belongs to the Lord,
and he rules over the nations.

Yea, to him shall all the proud of the earth bow down;
before him shall bow all who go down to the dust,
and he who cannot keep himself alive.
Posterity shall serve him;
men shall tell of the Lord to the coming generation,
and proclaim his deliverance to a people yet unborn,
that he has wrought it.

Psalm 31 (30)

In thee, O Lord, do I seek refuge;
let me never be put to shame;
in thy righteousness deliver me!
Incline thy ear to me,
rescue me speedily!
Be thou a rock of refuge for me,
a strong fortress to save me!

Yea, thou art my rock and my fortress;
for thy name's sake lead me and guide me,
take me out of the net which is hidden for me,

for thou art my refuge.
Into thy hands I commit my spirit;
  thou hast redeemed me, O Lord, faithful God.

Thou hatest those who pay regard to vain idols;
  but I trust in the Lord.
I will rejoice and be glad for thy steadfast love,
  because thou hast seen my affliction,
  thou hast taken heed of my adversities,
and hast not delivered me into the hand of the enemy;
  thou hast set my feet in a broad place.

Be gracious to me, O Lord, for I am in distress;
  my eye is wasted from grief,
  my soul and my body also.
For my life is spent with sorrow,
  and my years with sighing;
my strength fails because of my misery,
  and my bones waste away.
I am the scorn of all my adversaries,
  a horror to my neighbors,
an object of dread to my acquaintances;
  those who see me in the street flee from me.
I have passed out of mind like one who is dead;
  I have become like a broken vessel.
Yea, I hear the whispering of many —
  terror on every side! —
as they scheme together against me,
  as they plot to take my life.

But I trust in thee, O Lord,
  I say, "Thou art my God."
My times are in thy hand;

deliver me from the hand of my enemies and
    persecutors!
Let thy face shine on thy servant;
    save me in thy steadfast love!
Let me not be put to shame, O Lord,
    for I call on thee;
let the wicked be put to shame,
    let them go dumbfounded to Sheol.
Let the lying lips be dumb,
    which speak insolently against the righteous
    in pride and contempt.

O how abundant is thy goodness,
    which thou hast laid up for those who fear thee,
and wrought for those who take refuge in thee,
    in the sight of the sons of men!
In the covert of thy presence thou hidest them
    from the plots of men;
thou holdest them safe under thy shelter
    from the strife of tongues.

Blessed be the Lord,
    for he has wondrously shown his steadfast love to me
    when I was beset as in a besieged city.
I had said in my alarm,
    "I am driven far from thy sight."
But thou didst hear my supplications,
    when I cried to thee for help.

Love the Lord, all you his saints!
    The Lord preserves the faithful,
    but abundantly requites him who acts haughtily.
Be strong, and let your heart take courage,
    all you who wait for the Lord!

Psalm 38 (37)

O Lord, rebuke me not in thy anger,
   nor chasten me in thy wrath!
For thy arrows have sunk into me,
   and thy hand has come down on me.

There is no soundness in my flesh
   because of thy indignation;
there is no health in my bones
   because of my sin.
For my iniquities have gone over my head;
   they weigh like a burden too heavy for me.

My wounds grow foul and fester
   because of my foolishness,
I am utterly bowed down and prostrate;
   all the day I go about mourning.
For my loins are filled with burning,
   and there is no soundness in my flesh.
I am utterly spent and crushed;
   I groan because of the tumult of my heart.

Lord, all my longing is known to thee,
   my sighing is not hidden from thee.
My heart throbs, my strength fails me;
   and the light of my eyes — it also has gone from me.
My friends and companions stand aloof from my plague,
   and my kinsmen stand afar off.
Those who seek my life lay their snares,
   those who seek my hurt speak of ruin,
   and meditate treachery all the day long.

But I am like a deaf man, I do not hear,
   like a dumb man who does not open his mouth.
Yea, I am like a man who does not hear,
   and in whose mouth are no rebukes.

But for thee, O Lord, do I wait;
   it is thou, O Lord my God, who wilt answer.
For I pray, "Only let them not rejoice over me,
   who boast against me when my foot slips!

For I am ready to fall,
   and my pain is ever with me.
I confess my iniquity,
   I am sorry for my sin.
Those who are my foes without cause are mighty,
   and many are those who hate me wrongfully.
Those who render me evil for good
   are my adversaries because I follow after good.

Do not forsake me, O Lord!
   O my God, be not far from me!
Make haste to help me,
   O Lord, my salvation!

Psalm 39 (38)

I said, "I will guard my ways,
   that I may not sin with my tongue;
I will bridle my mouth,
   so long as the wicked are in my presence."
I was dumb and silent,

I held my peace to no avail;
my distress grew worse,
  my heart became hot within me.
As I mused, the fire burned;
  then I spoke with my tongue:

"Lord, let me know my end,
  and what is the measure of my days;
  let me know how fleeting my life is!
Behold, thou hast made my days a few handbreadths,
  and my lifetime is as nothing in thy sight.
Surely every man stands as a mere breath!
  Surely man goes about as a shadow!
Surely for nought are they in turmoil;
  man heaps up, and knows not who will gather!

"And now, Lord, for what do I wait?
  My hope is in thee.
Deliver me from all my transgressions.
  Make me not the scorn of the fool!
I am dumb, I do not open my mouth;
  for it is thou who hast done it.
Remove thy stroke from me;
  I am spent by the blows of thy hand.
When thou dost chasten man
  with rebukes for sin,
thou dost consume like a moth what is dear to him;
  surely every man is a mere breath!

"Hear my prayer, O Lord,
  and give ear to my cry;
  hold not thy peace at my tears!
For I am thy passing guest,

a sojourner, like all my fathers.
Look away from me, that I may know gladness,
   before I depart and be no more!''

Psalm 42 (41)

As a hart longs for flowing streams,
so longs my soul
   for thee, O God.
My soul thirsts for God,
   for the living God.
When shall I come and behold
   the face of God?
My tears have been my food
   day and night,
while men say to me continually,
   ''Where is your God?''

These things I remember,
   as I pour out my soul:
how I went with the throng,
   and led them in procession to the house of God,
with glad shouts and songs of thanksgiving,
   a multitude keeping festival.
Why are you cast down, O my soul,
   and why are you disquieted within me?
Hope in God; for I shall again praise him,
   my help and my God.

My soul is cast down within me,
   therefore I remember thee

from the land of Jordan and of Hermon,
   from Mount Mizar.
Deep calls to deep
   at the thunder of thy cataracts;
all thy waves and thy billows
   have gone over me.
By day the Lord commands his steadfast love;
   and at night his song is with me,
   a prayer to the God of my life.

I say to God, my rock:
   "Why hast thou forgotten me?
Why go I mourning
   because of the oppression of the enemy?"
As with a deadly wound in my body,
   my adversaries taunt me,
while they say to me continually,
   "Where is your God?"

Why are you cast down, O my soul,
   and why are you disquieted with me?
Hope in God; for I shall again praise him,
   my help and my God.

Psalm 51 (50)

Have mercy on me, O God,
   according to thy steadfast love;
   according to thy abundant mercy blot out my
      transgressions.

Wash me thoroughly from my iniquity,
   and cleanse me from my sin!

For I know my transgressions,
   and my sin is ever before me.
Against thee, thee only, have I sinned,
   and done that which is evil in thy sight,
so that thou art justified in thy sentence
   and blameless in thy judgment.
Behold, I was brought forth in iniquity,
   and in sin did my mother conceive me.

Behold, thou desirest truth in the inward being;
   therefore teach me wisdom in my secret heart.
Purge me with hyssop, and I shall be clean;
   wash me, and I shall be whiter than snow.
Fill me with joy and gladness;
   let the bones which thou hast broken rejoice.
Hide thy face from my sins,
   and blot out all my iniquities.

Create in me a clean heart, O God,
   and put a new and right spirit within me.
Cast me not away from thy presence,
   and take not thy holy Spirit from me.
Restore to me the joy of thy salvation,
   and uphold me with a willing spirit.

Then I will teach transgressors thy ways,
   and sinners will return to thee.
Deliver me from bloodguiltiness, O God,
   thou God of my salvation,
   and my tongue will sing aloud of thy deliverance.

O Lord, open thou my lips,
and my mouth shall show forth thy praise.
For thou hast no delight in sacrifice;
were I to give a burnt offering, thou wouldst not be
pleased.
The sacrifice acceptable to God is a broken spirit;
a broken and contrite heart, O God, thou wilt not
despise.

Do good to Zion in thy good pleasure;
rebuild the walls of Jerusalem,
then wilt thou delight in right sacrifices,
in burnt offerings and whole burnt offerings;
then bulls will be offered on thy altar.

Psalm 69 (68)

Save me, O God!
For the waters have come up to my neck.
I sink in deep mire,
where there is no foothold;
I have come into deep waters,
and the flood sweeps over me.
I am weary with my crying;
my throat is parched.
My eyes grow dim
with waiting for my God.

More in number than the hairs of my head
are those who hate me without cause;
mighty are those who would destroy me,

those who attack me with lies.
What I did not steal
   must I now restore?
O God, thou knowest my folly;
   the wrongs I have done are not hidden from thee.

Let not those who hope in thee be put to shame through
     me,
   O Lord God of hosts;
let not those who seek thee be brought to dishonor though
     me,
   O God of Israel.
For it is for thy sake that I have borne reproach,
   that shame has covered my face.
I have become a stranger to my brethren,
   an alien to my mother's sons.

For zeal for thy house has consumed me,
   and the insults of those who insult thee have fallen on
     me.
When I humbled my soul with fasting,
   it became my reproach.
When I made sackcloth my clothing,
   I became a byword to them.
I am the talk of those who sit in the gate,
   and the drunkards make songs about me.
But as for me, my prayer is to thee, O Lord.
   At an acceptable time, O God,
   in the abundance of thy steadfast love answer me.
With thy faithful help rescue me
   from sinking in the mire;
let me be delivered from my enemies
   and from the deep waters. . . .

Psalm 88 (87)

O Lord, my God, I call for help by day;
  I cry out in the night before thee.
Let my prayer come before thee,
  incline thy ear to my cry!

For my soul is full of troubles,
  and my life draws near to Sheol.
I am reckoned among those who go down to the Pit;
  I am a man who has no strength,
like one forsaken among the dead,
  like the slain that lie in the grave,
like those whom thou dost remember no more,
  for they are cut off from thy hand.
Thou hast put me in the depths of the Pit,
  in the regions dark and deep.
Thy wrath lies heavy upon me,
  and thou dost overwhelm me with all thy waves.
Thou hast caused my companions to shun me;
  thou hast made me a thing of horror to them.
I am shut in so that I cannot escape;
  my eye grows dim through sorrow.
Every day I call upon thee, O Lord;
  I spread out my hands to thee.
Dost thou work wonders for the dead?
  Do the shades rise up to praise thee?
Is thy steadfast love declared in the grave,
  or thy faithfulness in Abaddon?
Are thy wonders known in the darkness,
  or thy saving help in the land of forgetfulness?

But I, O Lord, cry to thee;
  in the morning my prayer comes before thee.
O Lord, why dost thou cast me off?
  Why dost thou hide thy face from me?
Afflicted and close to death from my youth up,
  I suffer thy terrors; I am helpless.
Thy wrath has swept over me;
  thy dread assaults destroy me.
They surround me like a flood all day long;
  they close in upon me together.
Thou hast caused lover and friend to shun me;
  my companions are in darkness.

Psalm 130 (129)

Out of the depths I cry to thee, O Lord!
  Lord, hear my voice!
Let thy ears be attentive
  to the voice of my supplications!

If thou, O Lord, shouldst mark iniquities,
  Lord, who could stand?
But there is forgiveness with thee,
  that thou mayest be feared.

I wait for the Lord, my soul waits,
  and in his word I hope;
my soul waits for the Lord
  more than watchmen for the morning,
  more than watchmen for the morning.

O Israel, hope in the Lord!
  For with the Lord there is steadfast love,
  and with him is plenteous redemption.
And he will redeem Israel
  from all his iniquities.

'I Am the Way. . .':
Holy Week Meditations

On the top of a hill called Calvary, outside Jerusalem, there were three crosses this Friday afternoon. They stood tall and ominous, silhouetted against the bleak, dark sky.

On this day at this hour, in a sense, time stood still. For on the center cross of heavy beams, with outstretched arms, hung crucified Jesus of Nazareth.

The executioners had driven hideous spikes through His hands — hands that had only blessed and helped people. And as He hung there now, covered with blood, His head crowned with ugly thorns, His face was contorted with pain and His body convulsed in agony. For three horrible hours He hung on that cross in excruciating pain.

Many in the crowd, empty-headed idiots, enjoyed the show of blood and tears. Some of them in their stupidity shouted out, "He saved others, let him save himself. Let him come down from the cross — and we will believe him" (see Matthew 27:40, Mark 15:29-31, Luke 23:35-37). Such vacuous-minded jeers were greeted with raucous laughter.

Christ on the cross whispered, "Father, forgive them, for they know not what they do" (Luke 23:34).

The rabble continued to rant, "He believed in God, let God now save him — if He will have him." Again, guffaws.

Jesus ignored the taunts. The criminal on His right was calling to Him for help. Hardly able to speak, the naked thief gasped, "Remember me . . . remember me . . . when you come . . . into your kingdom."

Jesus said, "This day you will be with me in paradise" (see Luke 23-43).

He could hardly say the words, yet He must reassure this dying man making this act of contrition. Then Jesus looked down and saw His dear Mother. His breathing was torture, every breath tremendously painful, His chest heaving violently for air; He had to draw himself up on the terrible spikes in His hands to gasp a little oxygen. Yet His thoughts were of others, as they had been all His life. He asked His beloved disciple John to take care of His Mother as his own (see John 19:27).

His blood dripped to the ground; His head was too heavy to hold up. His eyes became glazed. And then darkness gathered over all the landscape. Black clouds, angry and menacing, filled the heavens. Thunder rumbled warnings over the hills.

"Father," Jesus prayed, "I have finished your work — into your hands I commend my soul" (see Luke 23:46, John 19:30).

And the curtain in the temple was torn in two from the top to the bottom, and the earth quaked. Now when the centurion saw all this he fell to his knees and said, "Truly, this was the Son of God" (Matthew 27:54; see Mark 15:39; Luke 23:47).

A stranger in Jerusalem that day might have asked what this was all about: "Why did this man die?"

The people would have been hard-pressed to explain why. It didn't make sense to them either.

"Was he a robber or a murderer?" the stranger would ask.

"Oh, no. In fact, just the opposite."

"Was he a thief or a kidnapper?"

"Nothing like that."

"Then what was his crime?"

"Nothing. In fact, he went about doing good."

"That is considered a crime?"

"All I know," the other said, "is the reports I have heard and what I have seen. Everywhere he went he helped people. In Galilee in the north, and here in Judea in the south, he went from place to place healing and preaching. When people came to him for help — he never refused anyone."

"That to me sounds like a wonderful person, the kind we need more of in the world," the stranger commented.

"He was. He was a man of great unselfishness, and he taught that all of us should be unselfish too. He wanted a better world, a world where love would triumph over hatred. He said he came into the world to tell men that God is Love, and he wished to spread the love of God among the people. He said that the reason he was sent from God was that God so loved men that he wanted to put an end to their hostility."

"And they killed him for that?"

"It is hard to explain."

The stranger scratched his head and said, "It seems to me it is impossible to explain."

"That is true. It is impossible to explain," the local man said thoughtfully. He continued, "We first heard of him about three years ago. He was up in Galilee. That is where he is from — the village of Nazareth. He went from town to town preaching of the love of God. We have many rabbis who teach about God, but from the beginning, he was different.''

"How do you mean — different?''

"His message was so beautiful. He said we were all children of God and we should love one another as brothers and sisters. He said, when someone hit you — turn the other cheek. He told us to walk the extra mile, do good to those who persecute us.''

He went on: "Jesus spoke with authority. He did not quote others; he taught in his own name. And he said unusual but beautiful things like, 'Whenever you give a cup of cold water to anyone — you give it to me.' And he said, 'I am the way, the truth and the life.' And, 'Before Abraham came to be — I am.' And, 'The Father and I are one.' ''

"What did the people think of all this?'' the stranger asked.

"They flocked to him. He helped them. They loved him. He cured them physically and spiritually. He was the most generous person I have ever heard of. And then after he had spent the whole day with the people, he would often spend the whole night in prayer.''

"But,'' the stranger asked, "if the people loved him, why did they put him to death?''

"Oh, it was not the people, the ordinary people, who did this. They never knew anything about it until it was too late. It was our leaders who arrested him in the middle of the night, had the trial and had him on the way to Calvary this morning before the family people of Jerusalem were awake.''

"Didn't he have any followers?'' the stranger asked.

"Anyone who loves is his follower. He said this. He said, 'By this will all men know that you are my disciples — that you have love one for another.' '' (See John 13:35.)

This then could have been a conversation in Jerusalem on Good Friday, but there was more.

On Easter Sunday some of His followers went to the tomb, but the tomb was empty. These women rushed back and told the Apostles. Peter and John ran to the tomb and also found that it was empty. In the meantime, Mary Magdalene, one of the women, went back to the tomb alone. She knelt there crying, when someone asked her, "Why are you weeping?" She replied, "Because they have taken away my Master, and I don't know where they have laid him." Then, thinking this man was the gardener, she said, "Please tell me where you have taken him and we will get him and bury him privately and never bother you again."

But then the other said her name, "Mary." No one had ever pronounced her name as beautifully as Jesus, and so she knew it was Him, and she fell at His feet and said, "Master."

When Mary told the others, "I have seen the Lord," they would not believe her (see John 20:13-18).

But other things happened. Two disciples were on the way to the village of Emmaus, a short distance from Jerusalem. They were so saddened that when a stranger joined them they did not recognize Him. He asked them, "Why are you so sorrowful?" They replied, "You must be the only person in Jerusalem who does not know what happened to Jesus."

But then the stranger began to talk to them about the Scriptures, and how all the prophets had said that the Messiah must suffer for the people, and that His sorrow would give way to glory.

By this time they had arrived at Emmaus. The two were so encouraged and uplifted by the other's words they begged Him to stay and have supper with them at the inn. And at the supper, He "took the bread into his hands and, after saying grace, broke it into portions, which he gave to them," just as He had done at the Last Supper. It was in this "breaking of the bread" — the early Christians' term for the Eucharist — that at last the eyes of the two disciples were opened, and they recognized Jesus. And then He was no longer with them.

They said that surely they should have known who He was, because when He spoke to them of the Scriptures, "were not our hearts on fire?" They rushed back to tell the Apostles, but before they spoke, the Apostles said to them, "We have seen the Lord." Jesus had appeared to the Apostles also (see Luke 24:13-35).

The Apostles were filled with gloom after the death of Christ. They were hiding out in the upper room for fear the authorities would arrest them and punish them also. Every creaking sound on the stairs, as if someone were climbing them, made the Apostles shudder. The doors were locked, but then suddenly Jesus was standing in their midst. "Peace be to you," He said. After giving His followers His greatest gift on Holy Thursday, He gave another great gift. He who had forgiven sins constantly, now left this power with His followers, saying, "Whose sins you shall forgive, they are forgiven" (see John 20: 19-23). He never tired of giving gifts to us.

Thomas was not there that Easter afternoon. And when all the Apostles told Thomas, "We have seen the Lord," he was so stubborn he would not believe. In fact, he boldly proclaimed, "Unless I put my finger into his hand and my hand into his side, I will not believe."

The next time that Jesus came to them, Thomas was with them. Jesus said, "Peace be to you." Then He said to the doubter, "Come here, Thomas, and put your finger into my hand and put your hand into my side, and be not unbelieving but believing."

Thomas no longer doubted. He fell to his knees and said, "My Lord and my God!" (see John 20:24-29).

Later still the Apostles were fishing on the Lake of Galilee. They saw someone on the shore, but in the morning mist they did not know who it was. Then as they came closer, John said, "It is the Lord." The impetuous Peter could not wait but jumped into the water and swam to shore. And when they were all ashore, Jesus ate breakfast with them (see John 21:1-14).

At length it was time for Him to return to the Father. And so He said, "Go into the whole world, preach the Gospel to every creature, make disciples of all nations, baptizing them and teaching them to observe all that I have taught you" (see Matthew 28:19-20, Mark 16:15).

The "good news" Jesus brought into the world spread like a prairie fire to all the civilized nations. People everywhere soon knew about Jesus and His beautiful teachings. Many accepted His message and "put on Christ" (see Romans 13:14). They were baptized, for they found that what He had said struck a chord in their hearts. It was something they had always been looking for, and so love began to permeate their actions. In their blind search for the answer to the meaning of life they found Christ and His way of love, and joy filled their hearts.

Jesus with mildness and meekness had, like a lamb, accepted being scourged and crucified, pierced through and killed, but in doing so and in the Resurrection He conquered the hatred and evil that had put Him to death. His persecutors had not destroyed Him; He had destroyed their goal of preventing the spread of the "good news."

People became His followers; they became Christ-bearers and carried Christ to others. They learned of Christ and found that to know Him is to love Him, and they then passed on His love and carried on His work.

Christians sought to be peacemakers in a world of hostility. Jesus was the Prince of Peace. The first message of the angels at His birth was, "Peace on earth to men of good will" (Luke 2:14). In His first sermon, Christ said, "Blessed are the peacemakers, for they shall be called the children of God" (Matthew 5:9).

"Peace on earth" is the goal of every Christ-follower: peace among nations, peace between neighbors, peace in the home, peace in our hearts.

The peacemaker must be humble. This lesson we learn in the very beginning. It is interesting to observe who came to honor the Child born in the cave at Bethlehem, and it is equally interesting to note who did not come.

The shepherds came because they were unlearned and knew they did not know, and so when the angel announced the birth at Bethlehem, they went at once to honor the Child. And the wise men came because they were scholars and knew how little they knew. They made the long journey across the desert and knelt at the feet of the Child.

Who did not come that first Christmas? The proud people. The pseudo-intellectuals in Jerusalem, just a few miles away, did not come. Even if an angel had announced the news to them, they were too "learned" to go to the cave and kneel before a baby. The proud, with their sophomoric minds ("wise fools"), are with us still, of course. The humble today, as the humble in every age, have knelt to Christ. The proud of heart, like the haughty and pompous Pharisees, were too egotistical to honor anyone else.

The humble, like little children, are not all-knowing,

and they realize that to be near God one must become childlike in spirit. As Jesus said, "Unless you . . . become as little children, you shall not enter the kingdom of heaven" (Matthew 18:3; see Mark 10:15, Luke 18:17).

Like children we must be simple, loving, trusting; we must place our hope and faith in God with wholehearted abandonment, as little children trust their parents. "I have calmed my soul like a weaned child in its mother's arms," the psalmist tells us (Psalm 131:2).

Evil comes from growing away from the simplicity of the child; pride is the invention and the weakness of the ignorant human. And with pride, man twists good, pollutes the world and profanes the teaching of God. It is man who "fouls his nest." It is humans who make a criminal world, and to rectify this evil, Christ came — Christ who was misunderstood, mistreated, betrayed, beaten, deserted and hung on a cross to die. All this because He dared to bring the love of God into the world.

And yet many will not listen to Christ even today. To be popular with the crowd, one must turn his back on Christ; to mingle with the multitude who only believe in man, one can have no time for God. The crowd does not like thinking — it is too tiring — but the crowd is also unhappy, empty, heartsick and miserable.

The Christian chooses Christ and joy. With childlike faith, he kneels before Jesus. He recalls the words of our Lord, "I praise you, Father, Lord of heaven and earth, because you have hidden these things from the wise and prudent and have revealed them to your little ones" (Matthew 11:25, Luke 10:21).

The true Christian comes to know Christ, as superficial or nominal Christians never do. It is so easy to walk out on someone you do not know. In learning of Christ through prayer, the true Christ-follower sees a Person like no other person this world has ever known — One who with a glance could touch souls, who with a word could make men drop everything and follow Him. He loved sinners. His special interest were the sick and the sick of heart. He restored well-being to both. Often He did not even wait to be asked. His heart spontaneously went out to the suffering.

Jesus said, "Heaven and earth will pass away, but my word will not pass away" (Luke 21:33). He could change hearts and fire souls with zeal; He could make dull minds bright and cowards courageous. And no one prayed with the power Jesus did. His prayer was always, "[My will is] to do the will of him who sent me" (John 5:30). He said to His followers, "When you pray do not say many words as the pagans do" (Matthew 6:7). And He said, "When you pray, if you have anything against your neighbor, forgive him — so that your Father will also forgive you" (see Mark 11:25).

See Jesus standing in the square in Jerusalem when suddenly a woman, caught in the act of adultery, is thrown at His feet by the Pharisees. The hooting crowd has brought her, dragging her through the streets, and now pushes her at Him, and she on her knees is weeping and hiding her face.

To be caught in the act of adultery was death for the woman, according to the law then in Jerusalem.

Though more than once Jesus had said that adultery was a detestable sin, His heart went out to this weak and suffering woman. And He scorned the proud and haughty men standing about, who regarded themselves better than this contrite soul. They jeered at her, waiting for the excitement of stoning her to death to start. But Jesus did nothing, and the mob became silent and sullen, pouting like little kids.

Slowly Jesus stooped down and began writing with a stick in the sand. The Bible does not tell us what He wrote; but more than likely He was writing the names of sins — and the group of men gasped because the sins were theirs, their secret sins. Jesus exposed the sewer-like souls of these bold accusers who were brazenly pointing the finger of guilt at the woman. Jesus stood up and said, "Let him who is without sin cast the first stone."

Then he stooped again and began to write, and the men silently departed, deeply fearful that he was now going to write their names beside their sins. When He next stood up, no one was there except the woman.

Jesus said, "Is there no one here to condemn you?"

Her heart was in her mouth; she could not speak. Seconds before, she thought that she was going to be stoned to death. When at length she recovered her voice, she said, "No one, Lord."

"Then neither do I condemn you. Go in peace and sin no more."

At first she could not comprehend this, and then she realized He was letting her go free. She could hardly see His face for her tears. She wished to thank Him, but she didn't know how. But He seemed to understand. She wished to explain that it was not entirely her fault; her soul was weak and her lips beautiful, and she was poor — and men took advantage of her. But as she looked into His soulful eyes, she knew no explanation was necessary. She began to sob, and when she looked up again, He was gone (see John 8:3-11).

Jesus loved people — more than His own life. He loves each one of us more than words can tell. Because He loves us so much, He instituted the Eucharist so that He could always remain with us and could come into our hearts to dwell with us.

Jesus said, "I am with you always, even until the end of the world" (Matthew 28:20). He is with us, each of us, here and now. And once we open our hearts to Him, He is all that we need. "My grace is sufficient for you," He told St. Paul, "and my strength is made perfect in weakness."

Jesus could have been rich, but He was poor; He could have been powerful but chose to be a servant. He lived in times of great harshness, but He was exceedingly tender. No matter how little we love Him — He loves us with a great love. He loves us more than we can ever love. He is our Brother, constantly searching us out, waiting patiently for us to give Him a glance. We endure no pain, trouble, suffering, or difficulty that He is not there beside us. And He heals our wounded hearts. "Peace I leave with you; my peace I give to you; not as the world gives do I give to you" (John 14:27).

If we accept His love, we come to see that "others are Christ." We are not true to Him if we are obsessed only with our own salvation. To be a Christ-follower means to be like Christ, to be a giving person.

If we are rooted in Christ we will help others as He did. We, like Him, must reach out to the suffering, the hungry, the exploited, the imprisoned, the sick, the dying, and to those who do not know Jesus.

In the words of Jesus we say, "Thy kingdom come . . . on earth as it is in heaven" (Matthew 6:10). And we must make that kingdom come; it is a kingdom of love. We are making a mockery of what we say in the Our Father if we sit around and twiddle our thumbs and do nothing. A Christian is an activist. We must roll up our sleeves, if we are to please Jesus, and pitch in and do something, confident of Christ's help, for He said, "Let not your hearts be troubled" (John 14:1).

As a baptized person I have been called by Christ to play a role in making a better world. No one else can do it for me. A Christian is a candle that lights the darkness. The world needs Christ desperately, for there never was a time more cut off from Him than ours, nor one that needs Him more.

But despite our troubled world, the Christian is an optimist, for Jesus is with us, and Jesus said, "Fear not, I have overcome the world" (John 16:33).